Fundamentals of
Radio Broadcasting

Fundamentals of Radio Broadcasting

John Hasling
Foothill College

McGraw-Hill Book Company

New York St. Louis San Francisco Auckland Bogotá Hamburg
Johannesburg London Madrid Mexico Montreal New Delhi
Panama Paris São Paulo Singapore Sydney Tokyo Toronto

This book was set in Times Roman by National ShareGraphics, Inc. (ECU).
The editors were Richard R. Wright and James R. Belser;
The production supervisor was Donna Piligra.
The cover was designed by Robin Hessel.
The drawings were done by J & R Services, Inc.
R. R. Donnelley & Sons Company was printer and binder.

FUNDAMENTALS OF RADIO BROADCASTING

1 2 3 4 5 6 7 8 9 0   D O D O   8 9 8 7 6 5 4 3 2 1 0

Library of Congress Cataloging in Publication Data

Hasling, John.
    Fundamentals of radio broadcasting.

    Bibliography: p.
    Includes index.
    1. Radio broadcasting. 2. Radio stations.
I. Title.
PN1991.5.H3   384.54'023   79-18443
ISBN 0-07-026992-0

To Elsie . . .
for her loving support and encouragement

Contents

CONTENTS

Preface

Radio has been an important part of my life as far back as I can remember. Long before I entered the field professionally, I was an avid consumer. Just like so many others in my generation, I sat with my ear glued to the radio speaker, not wanting to miss even a single note of the opening theme music. The fact that I usually knew precisely what was going to be said, or what was going to happen, did not cause my interest to wane. There were certain events that always evoked laughter no matter how frequently they occurred—Jack Benny starting his Maxwell, Red Skelton playing the mean little kid, and Fibber McGee opening the door to his hall closet. Week after week I experienced the terror of *Inner Sanctum* and the excitement of *I Love a Mystery* just like millions of other Americans all over the country.

We were called the "great, unseen audience" because we were visible neither to the performers nor to each other. Yet we played a very important role in every scene—we designed and constructed the sets in our own imaginations. In doing so we were as much a part of the productions as any of the actors or directors, even though we were not aware of it. Reflecting upon this years later, I realized that one of the best schools of broadcasting was the radio set itself. All the people who are now creating the sounds we hear on the air began their careers by listening—not just using radio as a background for other activities, but "tuning in" to the content and to the ways programs are made.

I entered radio professionally after the "golden age" had ended. The "big bands" were starting to get smaller, and most of the top performers had moved to television. Most radio stations had begun to adopt the "music and news" format. But even in the early fifties there were still some "live" shows that appealed to small, select audiences. For the most part they originated at local stations, but they simulated the traditional formats of the network programs, with theme music and elaborate introductions. My first job was at KRE in Berkeley, California, while I was attending the University. I teamed with a classmate to do a program of college news that was called *Campus Capers*. From there it was on to even bigger things at KUKI, Ukiah, California (population 7,000). The pay was low and the hours were long, but the rewards were many. Our program director had a genius for adaptation—he took every idea that had ever been tried on radio and gave it his own special twist. The local audience loved it, because it seemed new and original. We would broadcast the Grange Hall dances, the Firemen's Ball, Little League baseball, and the city council meetings. Our election night coverage was as complex as that of the networks, complete with "live" reports from every precinct. All of us who worked at the station had a chance to do whatever our talents permitted—children's programs, talk shows, and original drama. It was hokey, but it was great fun; and it provided me the best experience I ever had in radio.

My fondness for small-market radio prevailed and spoiled me for the more rigid formats of the bigger stations. When I moved on to larger metropolitan areas, I earned more money but had far less latitude. The affluent stations had better equipment, a smoother sound, and more listeners, but there was less variety in programming. For that reason I chose to leave radio and enter the teaching profession. It was in the atmosphere of college radio that I again found the occasion for creative broadcasting.

Noncommercial and educational radio afford excellent opportunities for beginners in broadcasting. There is freedom to try whatever you want without the fear of losing sponsors, revenue, or your job. There is also the chance to participate in each of the various departments and apply all the talents you have. My plea to college and high school radio stations is to avoid falling into the trap of conformity that has been so pervasive among commercial stations.

The material for this book has been gleaned from many years of experience and contact with commercial and noncommercial stations. As an instructor of radio broadcasting at Foothill College, I have had a chance to keep up with modern radio programming practices. I have helped my students find employment in the field, and I have learned from them what is being demanded by broadcasting stations. I have tried to teach what students need to know to get jobs, and what station managers want from prospective employees.

This book is directed to students who are planning to work in college or community radio stations and to those who might be considering broadcasting as a career. It tells them what job opportunities are available and what kind of preparation is necessary. I encourage students to become familiar with as many facets of the business as possible. In this way they not only will be more attractive candidates for employment, but will derive greater enjoyment and satisfaction from the profession.

Working in radio is fun—there is no question about it. But the student of broadcasting must also be aware of the responsibility. Even a low-powered station has the potential of reaching tens of thousands of people. Anyone who opens a microphone must recognize the power and influence that radio has. An announcer or disk jockey can speak to as many people in one day of normal operation as the average person is able to reach in a lifetime. And one never knows who in the audience is going to listen and act upon what is said.

There is much to be learned about the broadcasting profession. It is my hope that this book will provide for the student the incentive to begin.

John Hasling

Acknowledgments

All books are products of many minds. The thoughts, ideas, and information I have put on these pages have come from more sources than I can possibly remember. I would have to begin by mentioning all the people with whom I worked at the radio stations where I was employed—KRE, Berkeley; KROG, Sonora; KUKI, Ukiah; KGMS and KCRA, Sacramento. Some of the people who were especially influential in my early years of broadcasting I have not seen for a long time—they may not even know how they impacted my life. Don Hambly and Bill Dyer were the ones who got me started in the business; Bill Ogden saw me through the license exam and is one of the best teachers I have ever known; John Franklin taught me what programming was all about; and Jack Matranga gave me the break that changed the direction of my career.

In the first several years after I entered the teaching profession I thought I had left behind all of my contact with radio broadcasting. I found myself back in the middle of it in 1971, when I was assigned the responsibility of faculty advisor to KFJC at Foothill College. It required of me a great deal of retooling and I learned much from my students in the process. Those in particular to whom acknowledgment is due are Ed Ely, Ross Forbes, Jona Denz, Rock Dibble, Sue Birge, Ron Teel, and Ken Forsyth.

The writing of this book provided me with the opportunity to visit radio stations, talk to the personnel, and take pictures. This was a valuable experience for me personally and contributed much to the book. I would especially like to thank stations KPEN, Los Altos; KXRX and KLOK in San Jose; KMEL, KMPX, KNBR, and KSFO in San Francisco; KKIS and KDFM in Walnut Creek; KSMC, Moraga; KOBO, Yuba City; and KARA, Santa Clara.

Appreciation is also extended to the companies which provided the photographs and materials that have been used to illustrate this book: RCA, Ampex Corporation, United Press International, Cetec Broadcast Group, International Taptronics Corporation, Job Leads, and the InterCollegiate Broadcasting Corporation. My thanks are also extended to Wayne Fogle and David Welch for their help with the photography.

I was fortunate in having excellent reviewers who provided insightful critiques and offered valuable suggestions—many of which were incorporated into the text. I have great respect and appreciation for the work done by Professor Marguerite A. Donnelly, St. John's University, New York; Paul W. Kelly, Fullerton College; and Howard A. Peth, Mt. San Antonio College.

John Hasling

Fundamentals of
Radio Broadcasting

Chapter 1

A Career in Radio

THE ADVANTAGES OF A CAREER IN RADIO

At this point your interest in radio broadcasting may be only a casual one. By reading this first chapter you should be able to decide if you want to continue on or forget the whole thing. There is a certain glamour to the broadcasting industry that makes it attractive as a means of making a living and expressing creative abilities. It is show business for the person unable to act, sing, dance, or play a musical instrument. It requires only that you be able to talk, and almost all of us can do that. But the simplicity is deceptive. There are relatively few people who have the combination of skills, talent, and desire to be successful broadcasters. Many who would be able to do it have chosen not to for a variety of reasons. We want to look at both the advantages and the disadvantages. Let's talk first about the positive side of the ledger.

Radio Is Contemporary

In every sense of the word broadcasting is a contemporary medium. It is in the forefront of new styles and modern trends. The nature of broadcasting lends itself to immediacy—getting the information first and making it available to the public in the shortest possible time. There is no need to set type or process film. The announcer needs only to open a microphone and speak. Fast-breaking news bulletins are usually heard first on radio, then seen on television. For this reason people have come to expect that radio will keep them always up to date. They will look elsewhere for historical perspectives and background material. Radio is the medium that tells them what is happening in the immediate present. The federal government's Emergency Broadcast System is predicated on the knowledge that most Americans will be listening to their radios at some time during the day. Therefore, emergency information can be transmitted to the entire population in a matter of minutes. Simultaneously, millions of people all over the country can receive an important news bulletin or a baseball score. A disk jockey will tell a joke, and thousands of people will laugh—individually, but together. But the following day everyone will have heard it, and the D.J. will have to come up with a new one. The materials of broadcasting, news, weather, and music are continually in flux, and broadcasters must always know what is current. It is their business to be aware of the movies, plays, concerts, lectures, sporting events, and cultural facilities that are available on a day-to-day basis in their communities. They are the source of information for contemporary social, commercial, and intellectual needs. The data they provide will influence conversation, attire, buying habits, and may also have an effect upon their listeners' musical tastes and political opinions. Radio broadcasting holds a strong appeal for the person who has wide interests in modern life and desires to be in the avant-garde.

Radio Is Creative

For the people performing routine jobs in commercial stations, to speak of the creative aspect of broadcasting may appear to be unrealistic. But the potential is there for the person who has new and imaginative ideas. In some respects there are more possibilities for creativity in radio than there are in television. Radio broadcasting is much less expensive; innovations can be tried without huge financial investments. Many cities have noncommercial or educational stations that are not dependent upon the support of sponsors. These outlets can risk loss of audience for the sake of trying something different. Radio does not require the elaborate special effects that are necessary for a television production. There is no need for costumes or sets; music and sound effects are inexpensive and can be produced in almost any small recording studio. This means that students and small broadcasters are not barred financially from creative expression. They are limited only by the dimensions of their talent and desire. While most radio drama has disappeared from the airwaves, there still is some left. In recent years there has been a renewed interest in the old radio shows, and it is not uncommon to hear the familiar themes and voices of *Ma Perkins, Lum and Abner,* and *The Shadow* being rebroadcast by local radio stations. While nostalgia was originally the primary motivation, recently there has also developed an interest in new and original radio drama. Much of this is being heard on public broadcasting stations (noncommercial) and college radio. But commercial stations are also programming some new drama. The most prominent, perhaps, is the *CBS Mystery Theater* which uses the "old-radio" format but puts the stories in more contemporary times. KSFO, a commercial station in San Francisco, offers *College Theater of the Air* once a week. They invite college radio workshops to produce original dramas and then come to record them at the KSFO studios.

Another creative form that is ideally suited to the medium of radio is oral interpretive reading. The most famous exponent of this art was Charles Laughton who toured the world telling stories and reading excerpts from great works of literature. Most colleges have courses in interpretive reading. These, combined with the talents of those who write for school literary magazines, could result in some extremely creative radio programming.

Radio Is Financially Healthy

There are more radio listeners today than there ever have been in our history. Also, people are listening longer—on the average about 3½ hours per day—just slightly less than the amount of time spent watching television.[1] The result is that advertisers are buying more radio air time than ever before. Radio is cheaper and reaches almost as many people as television. On radio the cost per listener is about 25 percent of what it is on TV, a bargain that business people cannot afford to pass up. Capital earnings of radio broadcasters are growing at a tremendous rate, and the cost of purchasing a radio station is increasing. Some are selling for as much as 16 million dollars. Salaries paid to radio personalities are also high—as much as $150,000 a year in some large metropolitan areas. There are, of course, stations that operate at the low end of the economic

---

[1] "Radio's Renaissance: Now It's Giving TV a Run for the Money," *U.S. News and World Report,* Jan. 16, 1978, pp. 49–50.

scale. Some of the small FM stations are low-budget enterprises and will pay disk jockeys only the minimum wage. But these are generally the places where neophytes get their experience. The high end of the scale is virtually unlimited, and even the middle-range salary is attractive. At the time of this writing the union-scale wage for a disk jockey on a medium-size station would be $300 to $400 a week. In addition to that, some are able to pick up extra money on the side by recording commercials for advertising agencies and making public appearances at dances and concerts.

Unions that represent broadcasting personnel are strong in some areas but not in others. There are several reasons for this. One is that being a disk jockey is an extremely attractive occupation, and a great many young people are willing to work for practically nothing, just for the privilege of being on the air. Another reason is that unions are unable to enforce job protection for broadcast personalities. A drop in a station's popularity rating has always been regarded as sufficient cause for firing a disk jockey. The personalities who are able to command a large listening audience are able to do their own negotiating with station owners without the help of a union. However, there are stations that do have union contracts. They usually are the high-powered AM stations in the large metropolitan regions. There are three nationally recognized unions for the broadcasting industry: The National Association of Broadcast Engineers and Technicians (NABET) is very strong in television but also represents some radio employees. The American Federation of Television and Radio Artists (AFTRA) is the union to be joined by announcers and performers who are not engineers or technicians. The International Brotherhood of Electrical Workers (IBEW) has a broadcast division and represents both radio and television workers. It is a union that is commonly joined by personnel who are performing the duties of both announcer and engineer.

Radio Is Prestigious

The job of disk jockey or announcer does not require a college degree, and radio performers enjoy considerable public prestige. There is a certain mystique connected to the broadcasting business. On the air you are reaching into the private lives of thousands of people. You may be an important part of their environment without ever knowing it. After listening to you for a long time people can develop a feeling that they really know you. When they meet you in person, there is naturally a great deal of interest and curiosity while they match their over-the-air impressions of you with the reality. Unlike the average citizen, who can remain fairly anonymous, as a radio personality you expose your knowledge, feelings, attitudes, and opinions for all to hear. You will have to get used to hearing yourself quoted and having your foibles, expressions, and anecdotes recalled to you by people you have never met before.[1]

THE REALITIES OF A RADIO CAREER

Radio is an attractive business for those who have the temperament for it. If you talk to someone who has a job as a radio announcer or disk jockey, you will probably get an enthusiastic response. For the most part the people who make a career of the broadcasting business do so because they love it. And the enthusiasm seems to be pervasive, even though the salaries are not always high. The stress produced by the pressures of the radio business makes it a profession that can be endured only by someone who is getting more out of it than just monetary rewards.

The Commercial Aspect

Consider first of all that broadcasting is essentially a commercial enterprise. While there are people who make a living in public broadcasting, they are relatively few in number. Most people in the profession are employed by commercial stations and networks. That is not true in all countries. Britain, for example, has an extensive public broadcasting system supported by tax money. The British Broadcasting Corporation is one of the most highly respected in the world, and, if you were a citizen of that country, you could work without having to contend with sponsors. (The British do have commercial broadcasting, but it is a separate entity from the BBC.) In the United States we have chosen to support our broadcasting stations through private enterprise. That means your primary task will be to *sell the product.* Your value to your employer will be measured in terms of how much you are able to contribute to increasing the sales of those who "buy time" from the station. After 15 years in the business one disk jockey summed up his career by saying that all he ever did was "move the beans off the shelf." You may be idealistic and reject such a notion. You may feel worthier working for a station that is "untainted" by commercials, but you must understand the realities of the business. It is difficult to support a family on the income afforded by a station that carries little or no advertising, because your salary is set in proportion to the income of your employer.

Even if you accept the commercial nature of radio, you may not be prepared for some of its abuses. As a disk jockey you will have to read all of the copy that is put in front of you. Some of it may annoy you. You may consider it to be degrading to the listener or even deceptive. But your job is not to make judgments; you are paid to sell the product. Many announcers have quit or been fired over this issue.

Job Security

Job security is another factor that you should consider before entering the field of radio. If you are the kind of person who likes to stay in one place for long periods of time, the business may cause you some unhappiness. While there is a certain amount of job security for engineers, air personalities tend to move or be moved frequently from one station to another. Every disk jockey plans on being fired at least once; some, several times. This is not necessarily a matter of professional competence. Employers realize this and do not hesitate to hire someone who has just been fired from another station. Longevity is not really a helpful professional attribute. A station manager does not expect announcers to stay more than a few years. The manager wants them to move on because their material begins to get stale. The announcer usually likes to move because moving offers gains in experience and professional growth.

Salary

If you are planning to stay in the radio business for a while you will want to think about raises and promotions. Starting salaries are generally good at AM stations, particularly those in metropolitan areas. But it is difficult to negotiate a raise above the union wage scale. At many stations you will have to lay your job on the line; then you may get what you want if the boss thinks you are a valuable property. If not, there are a dozen other people who would like to have your job, and remember, longevity is not considered to be an asset by most employers. Promotions, too, are hard to obtain. You may get to be program director, but, unless you have a strong business background, it is not likely that you will go beyond that. Station managers are usually selected from the ranks of the sales department. Naturally the job of chief engineer will go to someone who has technical knowledge and experience.

Social Life

There is one other factor you may want to keep in mind, and that is your social life. Radio stations are usually on the air twenty-four hours a day, seven days a week. You will have to expect that, frequently during your career, you will be working on weekends and holidays. When other people are out partying, it will be time for you to go to work. While radio may be exciting for you in the first few years, it begins to get tiresome to work every Christmas and New Year's Eve. Some people like it; others do not. Decide first what kind of a person you are, and if a career in radio will be consistent with your desired life-style.

JOBS IN RADIO

There are a variety of jobs you can pursue in the broadcasting business. Generally they fall under the headings of engineering, programming, news, and sales. The head of each department would have the title of *chief engineer, program director, news director,* or *sales manager.* An organizational chart might look something like that shown in Figure 1-1.

Announcer

The job in radio that probably comes to your mind first is that of an announcer. This is a term generally applied to well-known personalities who are heard on the network stations. Some of the larger local stations will also hire what are called "staff announcers." These are people who are generally employed because of the quality of their voices and their ability to read copy in a well-modulated tone. They are usually very highly paid professionals and have been in the broadcasting business a long time. Often they are actors, such as E. G. Marshall, or comedians, such as Gary Owens. This is not where *you* would start *your* broadcasting career.

Combo Operator

Most of the people who talk on the radio and play records call themselves disk jockeys. And a majority of the disk jockeys you hear are *combo operators.* The term *combo* means *combination announcer and engineer.* Most stations operate combo because the alternative is to hire two people instead of one, and that, of course, is much more expensive. The two-person arrangement is called *dual operation,* and a few stations still maintain it. It allows the station to hire a big-name personality without requiring him or her to have a license or engineering skills. But the job that you would most likely apply for is that of a combo operator. To obtain this position you would need to meet the following requirements:

1 *Have a radiotelephone operator's license.* Some stations require a first class license, which is very difficult to obtain and calls for extensive knowledge of electrical theory. Most require only a third class license or a restricted permit. We shall discuss how to obtain them in a later chapter.

2 *Know how to fill out program logs.* The program log tells what

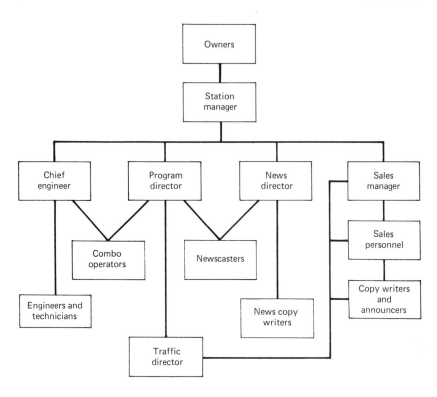

Figure 1-1 A medium-size radio broadcasting station will have an organizational structure similar to the one illustrated here. The station manager is responsible to the owner and provides direction for the four major departments—engineering, programming, news, and sales. The program director must work closely with the news director and sales manager and feed information to the traffic director. Note that the combo operators are responsible to both the chief engineer and the program director.

programs and spot announcements have been scheduled for the day. It is a guide for the combo operator and also serves as a record of what the station has put on the air. Keeping the log is not difficult, but it is an important part of the job. The Federal Communications Commission requires that logs be kept on file for 2 years and that they be available for public inspection.

3 *Know how to operate the equipment.* The combo person will be working with an audio console, turntables, tape recorders, and other equipment that will be described in later chapters. He or she will get on-the-job training but should have some basic knowledge of fundamental operations.

4 *Be able to speak in a clear, well-modulated voice.* The combo operator should be able to extemporize *(ad lib)* and also be able to read the printed word in a voice that sounds intelligent and conversational. The combo operator who aspires to be a "personality" disk jockey must also have a quick wit, a gift for gab, and some knowledge of records and performers.

Newscaster

Almost all stations broadcast some type of news. Generally the news is read by someone other than the disk jockey. If the station employs separate news personnel, the management will expect something more than just the ability to read copy. A newsperson on a radio station will be employed because he or she knows how to *write* copy as well as read it. A job in the news department may be much more exciting and challenging than a job as a disk jockey. For one thing you will get to read your own copy rather than that which has been written for you. You will also get a chance to talk to people and find out what is happening firsthand from those who are making the news. In order to fill this job you must be the kind of person who can work under pressure and meet deadlines. You may need the ability to read copy "cold" in case someone hands you a bulletin at the last minute. And, of course, you would have to be the kind of person who keeps up on current events and has a sense of responsibility for the public's right to know what is happening. Knowing how to type is a *must*. Also necessary is the ability to construct clear, concise sentences. Perhaps most important of all is to be able to make judgments as to which stories are most significant and most appropriate.

Salesperson

The people in the sales department are the ones who keep the station going financially. Also they probably will be the ones who are most highly paid. It is not at all uncommon for a good salesperson to be earning more than the program director or even the station manager. The salesperson makes contacts with the local merchants and arranges contracts for a certain number of spot announcements to be run on the station at certain times of the day. Sales personnel usually work on a commission basis but may also earn a salary. They may have other duties in addition to selling. Many times they will write the copy for their accounts, and occasionally do the announcing and production work as well. A member of the sales staff might also be doing a disk jockey show or working on promotion campaigns. This type of position is definitely one that you should consider as an entry into a broadcasting career, not just because it is lucrative, but because there are probably more job opportunities in sales than in any other aspect of the business.

Copywriter

Radio stations consume copy voraciously. A medium-size station that maintains an active news department may employ a dozen or more copywriters, just to feed material to the newscasters. In addition, copywriters are employed in the sales department to write commercial spot announcements. Again, the ability to type would be an important qualification, along with some facility in spelling and sentence construction. As a copywriter, you would need to be able to compose quickly, and often under considerable pressure.

Traffic Director

Although a disk jockey may be aware only of what is happening during a particular shift, or a newscaster may be concerned only with the reporting of current events, the traffic director knows what is happening at the station throughout the entire day. The traffic director is the individual who prepares the program log which will be followed by *all* on-the-air personnel. Based upon information received from the program director, the traffic director prepares the program log indicating which programs and commercials have been scheduled and the times they should be placed into the log. (See discussion of program logs in Chapter 7.) In addition to making entries in the log, the traffic director must be sure that the copy to be read and tapes to be played are placed properly for the use of an announcer, disk jockey, or newscaster.

Engineer

The engineering department is one that is extremely important to any broadcasting station. Maintaining the equipment so that it functions efficiently and with the necessary high fidelity is the essence of good radio station operation. Every station is required to have a chief engineer. This is the person who takes the responsibility of seeing that all the technical requirements of the station are met. The Federal Communications Commission demands that every broadcasting station operate within certain parameters. The chief engineer's job is to know precisely what these tolerances are and to see that the requirements are met. He or she must have a Radiotelephone Operator License First Class and must be familiar with the FCC's *Rules and Regulations.* The chief engineer must be able to do the maintenance on the transmitting equipment, as well as on the audio equipment in the studios. Small stations will probably have only one engineer, but larger ones will have several.

General Qualifications

There are a variety of talents and skills that can be useful in a broadcasting station. To prepare yourself for this career you will want to develop a broad background. Know as much as you can about all areas of the broadcasting business. The more things you can do, the more valuable you will be and the greater chance you will have for getting a job. While a college education is not required, the person with some academic background does have an advantage. Almost any course you might take could contribute to your value as a broadcaster, but some are more directly related to programming than others. Here is a list I would suggest.

Music appreciation	Acting
Public speaking	Sales and marketing
Voice and diction	Filmmaking
Oral interpretive reading	Journalism
Group discussion	Political science
English composition	Sociology

Students who take only broadcasting courses in college are limiting themselves considerably. They should have at least a smattering of knowledge about a variety of subjects.

In addition to the academic background, the person seeking a career in broadcasting needs experience. It is unrealistic to think that you will get your first job at a large station in a metropolitan area. You should plan on working for several years in small-market areas. If you are unwilling to move away from your home town, broadcasting is probably not the right career for you. You may also find that salaries are low in the beginning and that there are a lot of people who are willing to work for practically nothing at all. These are the realities with which you will have to contend.

SUMMARY

Just like any other business, broadcasting offers both advantages and disadvantages. It is a highly commercial industry, and the professional broadcaster must have a positive attitude toward the concept of advertising. Otherwise, pursuit of the career may lead to frustration and disillusionment. The radio business is contemporary, creative, prestigious, and sometimes lucrative. But the drawbacks should also be considered. While salaries are potentially high, they are generally low in the beginning. There is little if any job security, and working hours are often unattractive. Usually the person who pursues a career in broadcasting is one who is seeking a means of expression rather than just a method of making a living.

TERMINOLOGY

Ad lib
Audio console
AFTRA (American Federation of Television and Radio Artists)
BBC (British Broadcasting System)
Combo operator
Dual operation
EBS (Emergency Broadcast System)
FCC (Federal Communications Commission)
IBEW (International Brotherhood of Electrical Workers)
NABET (National Association of Broadcast Engineers and Technicians)
Program log
Radiotelephone operator license
Traffic director

ACTIVITIES

1 Find out how many AM and FM broadcasting stations there are in your area. Make a list of all the ones you are able to receive clearly on your own radio set. If you tune in on the hour you will hear the station give its call letters and location. List the call letters and get the address and telephone number of each of the stations.

2 Call a station that you like to listen to, and ask if you can come to visit. See if you can get a tour, and if possible talk to the station manager or program director. Find out what they consider to be the most important qualifications for a person entering the field of broadcasting.

The Development
of Radio Broadcasting

THE FIRST STEPS

The concept of contemporary broadcasting began with a memo written by David Sarnoff to the general manager of the Marconi Wireless Telegraph Company of America. The idea he expressed was to "bring music into the home by wireless."[1] This concept seems obvious to us now, but in 1915 it was a new idea. Radio had been born only 19 years before, when Guglielmo Marconi filed for a British patent on a device for the wireless transmission of telegraphic signals. Not until 1901 was the first radio signal sent across the Atlantic Ocean.

Before Sarnoff's memo, wireless transmission was seen as a point-to-point method of communication—one person to another. It had been used as a means of transmitting messages and news events, but to individuals, not to a broad audience. Furthermore, radio was conceived as

[1] Sydney W. Head, *Broadcasting in America* (Boston: Houghton Mifflin Company, 1972), p. 132.

an information, rather than an entertainment, medium. The only sound the system could produce was an unvarying tone. This was switched on and off to form the dots and dashes of Morse code, and in this way messages were sent and received. Those who knew the code and had receiving sets were few in number, and so David Sarnoff's memo seemed to suggest only a remote possibility. In order to send music into homes, a way had to be found to *modulate* wireless signals *with sound,* rather than merely chop them up into short electric impulses. This transmission system of sound-modulated radio frequency signals became known as *radiotelephone* communication. As early as 1908 Lee De Forest, an American inventor and pioneer in radiotelephony, broadcast phonograph recordings from the Eiffel Tower in Paris, and in so doing, became the first disk (rather, cylinder) jockey. In 1910 he attempted a broadcast with Enrico Caruso from the Metropolitan Opera House in New York, but microphones were then of poor quality and the voices were barely understandable.

By 1912 there were over a thousand amateur radio operators in the United States. In that year Congress passed the Radio Act, which was to be the first in a series of laws regulating radio communications. The Radio Act of 1912 proved to be ineffective because Congress had failed to make any provision for enforcement. Authority to administer the act was given to the U.S. Department of Commerce, but it had power only to issue licenses, not to establish rules and regulations. In 1920 broadcasting became a reality, putting even greater strain on the limitations of the Radio Act.

Commercial Development

There is some disagreement on the date and place of the first commercial broadcast. KQW in San Jose, California, began in 1909 and by 1912 was running regularly scheduled programs for a general audience. But the station often given credit for being first is KDKA in Pittsburgh, Pennsylvania. While there may have been others operating on a regular basis, KDKA was the first station to be issued a license by the Commerce Department for the specific purpose of broadcasting. The station was owned and operated by Frank Conrad, an engineer for the Westinghouse Corporation. Westinghouse was beginning to manufacture radio receivers and could see the possibilities in broadcasting. Dr. Conrad had been regularly playing phonograph records on the air and making announcements of various sorts, sometimes accommodating people who wanted to hear specific selections; this was perhaps the first request program. Westinghouse bought the enterprise and constructed a transmitter specifically for the purpose of broadcasting. On November 2, 1920, the new station, KDKA, went on the air with the returns of the Harding-Cox election—the first news report from a licensed broadcasting station.

But KDKA inaugurated another far-reaching concept. In addition to music and news, the station gave information about radio kits that were manufactured by Westinghouse and sold for $10 at Horne's Department Store. Radio commercials had been born.

GOVERNMENT REGULATIONS

By the mid 1920s it was clear that the Radio Act of 1912 was inadequate. After being licensed, stations were changing their power and frequency, and there was nothing the Commerce Department could do about it. Furthermore, the act did not make any provision for denying a license, and there were more applications than there were available channels. In 1923 the U.S. Supreme Court found that the Commerce Department had an impossible task, but it was not until four years later that there was new legislation.

In February 1927, a new Radio Act was passed—the first to recognize the concept of broadcasting. It established a five-member board, called the Federal Radio Commission (FRC), that was appointed by the President. Even more significantly, the Radio Act addressed itself to the philosophy the government was to maintain toward the radio industry. It acknowledged that broadcasting was a unique service; that the "airwaves" and the channels into which they were to be divided belong to the people; that not everyone was entitled to or could receive a broadcasting license; that broadcasting was a form of expression protected by the First Amendment; that service must be equitably distributed; and that the government had discretionary regulatory powers. Both the philosophy and the structure of this act were later incorporated into the Communications Act of 1934. The 1934 legislation will be discussed in more detail in Chapter 3.

THE GOLDEN AGE OF RADIO

The years that followed the Radio Act saw tremendous developments in broadcasting, culminating in what we now call the "golden age of radio." This prodigious period ranged from the late 1920s until the late forties when television began to dominate electronic entertainment. The golden age spanned two decades that were highlighted by lovable personalities, stalwart heroes, hilarious comedians, insightful commentators, creative drama, and sentimental music. Best of all to a nation of people struggling through a depression, it was all free. For many it was virtually the only form of entertainment available.

The Rise of the Networks

The commercial concept of broadcasting had been established by station KDKA and Westinghouse. There was money to be made in broadcasting, but it required the organization of big corporations. The first of the big networks, NBC, was formed in 1926 by RCA, General Electric, and American Telephone and Telegraph. It was actually two networks; AT&T operated what it called the Red Network, and RCA had the Blue Network. This arrangement was not only very confusing to the public, but to announcers as well. In 1927 the Columbia Phonograph Company incorporated what is now the Columbia Broadcasting System. This network was quite successful in increasing the fortunes of one of its advertisers, the Congress Cigar Company of Philadelphia. Its sales doubled in one year. The advertising manager of that company, William Paley, became intrigued by the success of CBS and began to devote his energies to broadcasting rather than to the marketing of cigars. He eventually became chairman of the board of CBS and retained the position for 50 years.

The networks were responsible for the memorable programs that were produced in the 1930s and 1940s. Local stations were not able to pay the large sums that were necessary to attract the big-name entertainers. Small stations had to rely on local talent and phonograph records, programming fare that could not hope to compete with the network shows. In the mid-1930s almost half of the existing broadcasting stations were affiliated with networks, and few of the others were making money. In addition to being responsible for the popularity of local stations, the networks made stars out of a number of small-time entertainers. Vaudeville was the training ground for the broadcasting studio, and almost any act that was adaptable to the sound medium was given a chance. Some of the acts had to be modified, such as that of a performer who had been billing himself as the World's Worst Juggler. He might have retained that title had he not changed his name to Fred Allen, abandoned juggling, and become a comedian. The networks tried whenever they could to advance the careers of talented people. Not for altruistic, but for monetary reasons. The public loved it when an unknown performer became a star. This social characteristic was responsible for the success of the *Major Bowes Amateur Hour,* which launched the careers of many performing artists as well as entertainers. Among them were Robert Merrill, Vic Damone, and Frank Sinatra.

It was difficult then as it is now to predict what combination of personalities would be a hit on radio. An important factor was the partnership. For some reason performers on radio seemed to do better in pairs. The evidence for this is Jack Benny and Mary Livingstone, Fred Allen and Portland Hoffa, George Burns and Gracie Allen, Fibber McGee and Molly, Bob and Ray, *Lum and Abner,* and the *Easy Aces.* Perhaps the most successful pair on radio were Freeman Gosden and Charles Correll, who in 1928 began syndicating a program called *Amos 'n' Andy.* For 20 years the series was one of the most popular programs on the air. Patrons in movie theaters would get up in the middle of a film to step into the lobby and listen to *Amos 'n' Andy.* While the two performers became legendary, their popularity terminated in the fifties as a result of the visual element introduced by television.

A Medium of Sound

Television was responsible for the demise of many programs that had been popular on radio. One factor was that characters in a drama often did not *look* the part. Sometimes heroes did not appear to be heroic, and heroines were not the gorgeous creatures described. Furthermore, sets were less elaborate. No television studio could ever devise a set that could compare to the one created in the imagination. The visual element put severe restrictions upon script writers. Considerably less can be done when images are confined to that which can be seen. On October 30, 1938, there occurred a phenomonon that could never be duplicated on television. It was the radio production of *The War of the Worlds.* When the characters in the Orson Welles drama began describing the invasion of the Martians, millions of people all over the country "saw" it in their minds, and this "staging" was more realistic than that created in *Star Wars.* Through the medium of sound, audiences could be transported instantaneously anywhere in the world. The only set designer needed was a sound effects man with a creative imagination. Scene changes were effected by means of musical "bridges"—short musical passages, a few seconds in length, that suggested transitions in time or space. Timing was an essential factor, because dramatic programs were seldom more than 30 or 60 minutes in length. Each program had to fit into the "block" of time allocated for it.

Block Programming

Block programming is a term used to refer to the policy of dividing the broadcast day into segments. At one time it was common practice, but today only a few stations select that option. Television retains the block programming concept, but not radio. Program blocks were usually in

15-, 30-, or 60-minute segments, and the time was sold in its entirety to a single sponsor. In the early days of broadcasting we spoke in terms of "radio programs," and each one was a separate unit, with its own introduction and conclusion. People would listen for the specific programs of their choice and were very much aware of the time that each one started.

There was also very strong sponsor identification during the days of block programming. Listeners were as familiar with the products advertised as they were with the performers on the program. The term "soap opera" was coined to refer to all of the human interest dramas that were sponsored by soap manufacturers. In those days listeners knew each brand of soap as well as they knew the characters in the drama. Often the announcer who read the commercial would have a role to play in the program. Sometimes he (almost always male) would serve as the narrator and, occasionally, as one of the personalities. Don Wilson, for example, was as much a part of the Jack Benny program as any of the other entertainers, but his primary function was to read the sponsor's message. The strong identification was very advantageous to the sponsor. The listener's loyalty to Jack Benny was extended to Don Wilson, and subsequently to Jell-O or to Lucky Strike or to whatever other product was advertised on the program.

The fact that radio has moved away from the block programming concept is a significant one. It has taken away the influence of the sponsor and put the responsibility for programming into the hands of the local station. In the early days of radio the sponsors made all the important decisions. They were the ones who decided whether a program would continue or be cancelled; they hired and fired performers and announcers. They provided the money and they had the power. Their 15- or 30- minute block of time was their own to do with as they wished. This is no longer the case. Radio stations sell air time on a *participating* basis. The advertiser buys only a spot announcement of one minute or less in length and has no control over the programming of the station. The change came about in the 1950s when stations began to realize that people were no longer listening to individual programs, but to the radio station itself. And they wanted the "sound" of the station to remain more or less consistent throughout the day. A modified form of block programming may be heard today on radio stations that choose to provide variety in the type of music that is offered. The segments may be several hours in length at a particular time of the day, and might feature concert, operatic, or "easy listening" music. Occasionally you may find a station that offers an advertiser the option of buying a block of time at a special rate, but, for the most part, commercial stations choose to program a consistent "sound" throughout the day and sell air time in short, spot announcements.

THE DEVELOPMENT OF FM

In the years after World War II a new dimension was added to radio broadcasting—frequency modulation. Along with the invention of radar during the war, considerable other development had been done with radio transmission in the very high frequency range. The Federal Communications Commission set aside the band from 88 to 108 megahertz (then called "megacycles") for commercial and noncommercial broadcast, utilizing FM transmission. FM produces sound of much higher fidelity than AM and was designed in the beginning as a music medium. While FM is limited in the distance it can cover, its superior sound quality and, now, stereo capability make it a most valuable medium of broadcasting. FM has a wider frequency band. It is measured in millions rather than thousands of cycles per second. There are two hundred thousand cycles between each FM channel and the next—an interval wider than the entire AM band. The wider range permits clearer tones in stereophonic as well as monophonic sound. Technology is now available to provide stereo on AM, but the quality will still not be as good as that on FM. Furthermore, some FM stations have begun to experiment with *quadraphonic* sound. These new developments will mean, of course, that new receiving sets (or, at least, adapting equipment) will have to be purchased by the public; this is one of the factors of marketing that has always played a part in the growth of the radio industry.

In 1945 there were only fifty FM transmitting stations in the country. There were not many receivers either, and advertisers were reluctant to spend money on commercial messages that would be heard by so few people.

Growth was rapid in the early years, and by 1949 there were 743 stations. But there was a decline after that, when FM stations failed to become as popular as had originally been expected. One reason was that recording facilities had not been able to match the quality of transmission. Live music sounded excellent on FM, but recorded music still left much to be desired. Sales representatives found it difficult to sell time on FM stations and continued to look to AM for financial solvency. Most FM stations were owned and operated by AM broadcasters who would simply duplicate the programming on both stations. This practice is called *simulcasting* and was quite common until the FCC put some restrictions upon it. FM limped through the fifties without coming close to the expectations of its founders.

In 1965 the picture began to change for FM. The FCC ruled that not more than 50 percent of its programming could be simulcast. Broadcasters began to sell their FM "outlets" to independent operators, and FM started to develop an identity of its own. At the same time, recording equipment had improved, stereophonic sound had become a reality, and the public was beginning to trade in its old equipment for new models. As the number of FM receivers increased, so did the financial climate of FM broadcasting. Today there are twice as many FM stations as AM, and the advertising dollar is shared about equally between the two.

PROGRAM CONTENT

Ever since the Radio Act of 1927, the federal government has had difficulty in defining its regulatory power over broadcasting. The Radio Act made clear that broadcasting was protected by the First Amendment and at no time was the FRC (later the FCC) intended to impose censorship upon radio stations. But difficult questions have arisen in regard to the broadcasters' responsibility to the public. One of these questions has to do with the matter of indecency. In the early 1970s radio talk programs became quite popular. At first the programs dealt with local and national issues, but as society became more permissive, the subject matter started to change. Topics on talk shows switched from social issues to sex. People who called in were quite willing to discuss the intimate details of their own sex lives. The public loved it and so did the broadcasters. Ratings soared on the talk stations. But at the same time, letters of protest began to flow in. Eventually the FCC had to take action. WGLD-FM in Oak Park, Illinois, was fined $2,000 for violating the FCC rule pertaining to obscene and indecent material. But the case was never appealed to the courts and the FCC ruling remains indecisive. In a more recent case, station WBAI-FM, in New York, was cited by the FCC for playing a recording by comedian George Carlin called *Seven Words You Can Never Say on Television.* This case went all the way to the Supreme Court, which ruled in 1978 that the FCC does have the power to impose fines on stations which broadcast material that is "patently offensive" and without socially redeeming value.

THE RADIO CODE

The question of government regulation over program content was one that was anticipated by broadcasters. In 1937 an organization was formed known as the National Association of Broadcasters. The purpose was to establish a self-regulatory agency to minimize the need for government intervention. The NAB framed a *Radio Code* and revised it in 1945. In the Radio Code, acknowledgment was made of the fact that standards for broadcasting can never be final or complete, but are subject to periodic revision as social attitudes and mores change. The position of code authority director was established to "maintain a continuing review of all programming and advertising material presented over radio . . . to receive, screen and clear complaints concerning radio programming . . . to define and interpret words and phrases in the Radio Code . . . [and] to develop and maintain appropriate liaison with governmental agencies. . . ."[2]

In addition the code prescribed for the quantity and quality of advertising, the treatment of children's programs, and the handling of controversial issues. Most broadcasters have found the NAB code to be reasonable and recognize the validity of its standards. Yet, membership in the association is voluntary, and some stations choose to set their own guidelines.

SUMMARY

Radio transmission spans a history of just over 80 years; broadcasting less than that. The names we will remember in the electronic phase are Marconi, Hertz, and De Forest; in programming and general development we will remember Sarnoff, Conrad, and Paley. The first corporations instrumental in radio's progress are Westinghouse, AT&T, General Electric, and RCA. The golden age of radio will always be a memorable period in the history of the United States, having contributed much to the entertainment and information needs of our citizens. FM has developed slowly but is now finally coming into its own. The ethics of the broadcasting industry will perhaps always be in question, and, as social standards change, there will be a continuing need for reevaluation.

TERMINOLOGY

Block programming	Radiotelephone
Broadcast	Simulcasting
Participating (advertiser)	Sound-modulated radio signal
Point-to-point communication	Sponsor
Quadraphonic	Stereophonic

ACTIVITIES

1 Visit your public library and see if it has a record collection of old radio programs. Listen for the sound effects and music bridges to see how the director sets the stage and brings about the transitions.
2 Buy a kit in a hobby store to make a crystal set. See how many stations you

[2] National Association of Broadcasters, *The Radio Code*, 1976, p. 21.

can pick up. Think of the progress that has been made in the development of radio receivers. Consider the quality of the sound and the difficulty in finding stations.

3 Write and produce a radio drama in the style of the old-time radio plays, using sound effects and music bridges. Record the production in a 15- or 30-minute block of time.

Government Regulation

THE COMMUNICATIONS ACT OF 1934

To operate a broadcasting station one must accept certain responsibilities that are not imposed on people in other businesses. The reason for this is that a broadcaster uses a public resource. The airwaves are not private property; they belong to us all. Channels upon which broadcasters operate are in limited supply, not available to everyone. Those who are granted permission to use a broadcast channel must accept the terms and conditions of the assignment. The legislation under which all broadcasters operate is the Communications Act of 1934. It adopted the tone and philosophy of the Radio Act of 1927 and added a few refinements, one of which was the creation of the Federal Communications Commission.

The Federal Communications Commission

The Federal Communications Commission (FCC) is composed of seven commissioners appointed by the President with the advice and consent of the Senate. The Communications Act provides that the Commission has the "authority to make general rules and regulations requiring stations to keep such records of programs, transmission of energy, communications, or signals as it may deem desirable."[1] Broadcasting stations are required to keep up-to-date copies of the *Rules and Regulations* and are expected to apply them in their day-to-day operation. The act also provides that the commission has "authority to inspect all radio installations associated with stations required to be licensed . . . to ascertain whether in construction, installation and operation they conform to the requirements. . . ."[2] For the convenience of FCC inspectors and the general public, each station is required to maintain a *public file,* which should contain the following:

1 The original application for the station license
2 The applications for license renewals
3 All applications for construction permits to modify facilities
4 Proof of performance; Verification that the station has been operating according to the technical specifications of the license
5 All correspondence with the FCC
6 Correspondence with the public that pertains to fulfilling programming responsibilities
7 Program and transmitter logs for the past 2 years
8 Maintenance logs; A record of adjustments and modifications made on transmitting equipment

The public file must be made available to an FCC inspector or any member of the general public upon request during normal business hours. It is one of the means the Commission uses to see that a station is operating within the terms of its license. In addition, the FCC may monitor a station and take measurements of its signal with electronic instruments.

VIOLATIONS

The creation of the FCC was significant because it provided a means of enforcing the rules that govern broadcasting. Before the 1934 Act there was very little that could be done to see that radio operators obeyed the laws. The FCC has the power to exercise considerable force upon broadcasters. In cases of minor infractions, fines can be levied on the holder of the license. When a rule violation has been identified, the FCC will issue

[1] Public Law 416, 73d Congress, June 19, 1934, sec. 303(j).
[2] Ibid., sec. 303(n).

a *citation.* The citation will specify which particular section of the *Rules and Regulations* has been violated. The station or individual must reply within 10 days and provide an explanation of the infraction. If the offense is minor, the FCC may require only that the condition be corrected. If it is more serious, a fine may be imposed or the license suspended. The station does however, have recourse. It can demand a hearing by the Commission and even take its case to the federal courts. This is an expensive procedure, of course, and not one that is often pursued.

RESTRICTIONS

The restraints put upon broadcasters are necessary and reasonable. Slander, of course, is actionable here as it is anywhere else. In addition, there are three sections of the Criminal Code that pertain directly to the broadcaster: those on lottery information, fraud, and obscenity.[3]

The Criminal Code

> *Section 1304. Broadcasting lottery information* Whoever broadcasts by means of any radio station for which a license is required by any law of the United States, or whoever, operating any such station, knowingly permits the broadcasting of, any advertisement of or information concerning any lottery, gift enterprise, or similar scheme, offering prizes dependent in whole or in part upon lot or chance, or any list of prizes drawn or awarded by means of any such lottery, gift enterprise, or scheme, whether said list contains any part or all of such prizes, shall be fined not more than $1,000 or imprisoned not more than one year or both.
>
> Each day's broadcasting shall constitute a separate offense. (Codified June 25, 1948, ch. 645, 62 Stat. 763.)

An exception to the above law has been passed in recent years in order to permit the broadcasting of state lotteries that are used for tax revenue purposes. But section 1304 is still applicable to private individuals and corporations.

> *Section 1343. Fraud by wire, radio, or television* Whoever, having devised or intending to devise any scheme or artifice to defraud, or for obtaining money or property by means of false or fraudulent pretenses, representations, or promises, transmits or causes to be transmitted by means of wire, radio, or television communication in interstate or foreign commerce, any writings, signs, signals, pictures, or sounds for the purpose of executing such schemes or artifice, shall be fined not more than *$1000* or imprisoned not

[3] Frank J. Kahn, *Documents of American Broadcasting* 2d ed. (Englewood Cliffs, N.J.: Prentice-Hall, 1973) pp. 112–113.

more than five years, or both. (Codified July 16, 1952, ch. 879, sec. 18(a), 66 Stat. 722; amended July 11, 1956, ch. 561, 70 Stat. 523.)

Section 1464. Broadcasting obscene language   Whoever utters any obscene, indecent, or profane language by means of radio communication shall be fined not more than $10,000 or imprisoned not more than two years, or both. (Codified June 25, 1948, ch. 645, 62 Stat. 769.)

A violation in any one of these cases, of course, would have to be determined in a court of law. Infractions can be brought to the attention of the FCC by any member of the public. Cases of obscenity are the most common, but also the most difficult to prosecute. The definition is not at all clear, and the Supreme Court has said that it depends upon "contemporary community standards." What is considered obscene in some areas may not be in others. The context in which the utterance takes place also seems to make a difference. Obscenity in the lyrics of a song is often considered less offensive than the same expressions uttered in prose. But remember that it is against the law, and you may want to ask yourself some questions about it: What would radio sound like if it were legal? How much are you willing to risk to press the issue?

SECTION 315

The basis of frequent discussion and controversy, section 315 of the Communications Act, pertains to the responsibilities of a broadcaster during political campaigns.

If any licensee shall permit any person who is a legally qualified candidate for any public office to use a broadcasting station, he shall afford equal opportunities to all other such candidates for that office in the use of such broadcasting stations: *Provided,* that such licensee shall have no power of censorship over the material broadcast under the provisions of this section. No obligation is imposed under this subsection upon any licensee to allow the use of its station by any such candidate. Appearance by a legally quali-fied candidate on any

1   bona fide newscast,
2   bona fide news interview,
3   bona fide news documentary (if the appearance of the candidate is coincidental to the presentation of the subject or subjects covered by the news documentary), or
4   on-the-spot coverage of bona fide news events (included but not limited to political conventions and activities incidental thereto),

shall not be deemed to be use of a broadcasting station within the meaning of this subsection. Nothing in the foregoing sentence shall be construed as relieving broadcasters, in connection with the presentation of newscasts, news interviews, news documentaries, and on-the-spot coverage of news events, from the obligation imposed upon them under this Act to operate in the public interest and to afford reasonable opportunity for the discussion of conflicting views on issues of public importance.[4]

The section goes on to explain that all candidates who buy time on a commercial station must be charged the same rate, and that the rate must be no higher than is normally charged by the station. Noncommercial stations which donate their time to candidates must provide equal time to all candidates for the same office. This section of the Communications Act has been strongly criticized on the ground that, contrary to its stated intent, its implementation actually hampers access of candidates to the media. Some stations will not give time to *any* candidate, arguing that they cannot afford to accommodate *every* person claiming to be a candidate for that office, as the "equal opportunity" clause would require. During presidential campaigns, stations are loath to give time for debates between candidates for the same reason. An exception to this was first made in the 1960 campaign, when the networks gave time for a series of debates between Richard Nixon and John Kennedy. But in order to do this, Congress had to suspend the rules of section 315 for the needed period of time.

THE FAIRNESS DOCTRINE

Originally the FCC intended that broadcasting stations should not take sides on controversial issues. Newspapers, of course, have always been free to editorialize; indeed, that has been one of their prime functions. But the status of broadcasters is different, because they use a public asset—the airwaves—as their medium of communication. The price of a printing press is all that is required to establish a newspaper and print whatever one wishes. But channels for broadcasting are few and access is not available so easily. All through the early years of development, broadcasters avoided issues that might be regarded as controversial. In 1949 that condition changed. The FCC issued the Fairness Doctrine, which stated, in effect, that stations could express opinions on matters of public importance as long as an effort was made to air all sides of the issue. At first broadcasters were reluctant to implement the new ruling for fear of offending sponsors and listeners. Then a few brave souls

[4] Ibid. p. 80.

began trying it out; now almost every commercial station you hear takes an editorial stand on some issues, or allows listeners to broadcast *free-speech messages.*

In 1964, 15 years after the adoption of the Fairness Doctrine, the FCC issued a *Primer* in an attempt to explain some of the ambiguities. In part it says:

> While Section 315 thus embodies both the "equal opportunities" require-ment and the fairness doctrine, they apply to different situations and in different ways. The "equal opportunity" requirement relates solely to use of broadcast facilities by candidates for public office. . . .
>
> The fairness doctrine deals with the broader question of affording reasonable opportunity for the presentation of contrasting viewpoints on controversial issues of public importance. Generally speaking, it does not apply with the precision of the "equal opportunities" requirement. Rather, the licensee, in applying the fairness doctrine, is called upon to make rea-sonable judgments in good faith on the facts of each situation—as to wheth-er a controversial issue of public importance is involved, as to what view-points have been or should be presented, as to the format and spokesmen to present the viewpoints, and all the other facets of such programming.[5]

While this language may appear to be extremely vague, there are several points upon which the FCC is clear. It establishes that, when a viewpoint is expressed on the air, the station must make a conscientious effort to seek out a spokesperson for the other side. When the viewpoint involves a personal attack upon an individual or an organization, the station is obliged to send a transcript of the message to the concerned parties and offer them equal time to reply. If a viewpoint is expressed on a campaign issue during an election period, the station must allow opposing candi-dates or their designated spokesmen to reply.

The Fairness Doctrine still has a number of ambiguities that will require clarification in the courts. There is a strong movement among broadcasters to abolish the doctrine altogether. We can expect that it will be subject to continued modification for many years to come.

Freedom of Expression

One of the most important parts of the Communications Act is section 326. The main paragraph reads as follows:

> Nothing in this Act shall be understood or construed to give the Commis-sion the power of censorship over the radio communications or signals transmitted by any radio station, and no regulation or condition shall be

---

[5] Ibid., pp. 395–396.

promulgated or fixed by the Commission which shall interfere with the right of free speech by means of radio communication.

While the Commission does require that stations submit their program schedules for approval, it does not specify what the programs should be. Everything in the Communications Act is designed to promote free expression rather than thwart it. But the Act does impose certain restrictions to protect the rights of those members of society who do not own broadcasting stations. In other words, broadcasters should not have an unfair advantage over everyone else. In fact, there has been a strong movement in recent years toward *public access* to the media. At the urging of the Commission, broadcasters are making a concerted effort to encourage members of the public to use the facilities of radio and television stations.

SUMMARY

The Communications Act of 1934 is the most significant piece of legislation affecting the broadcasting industry. Out of it came the Federal Communications Commission, which exercises control over all radio and television transmission. The Commission requires that anyone engaged in broadcasting activities be familiar with *Rules and Regulations,* a document that establishes the parameters for use of the airwaves. The airwaves are regarded as public property and therefore must be used in the public interest. While the Communications Act maintains that the FCC does not have the power of censorship, it does grant the Commission the ability to suspend licenses and impose fines. It also demands that broadcasters not use the airwaves to cheat, offend, or take advantage of the public. It insists that controversial issues and matters of public importance be dealt with fairly.

TERMINOLOGY

Airwaves	Logs
Channel	Primer
Citation	Proof of performance
Construction permit	Public file
Fairness Doctrine	*Rules and Regulations* (R & R)
Free-speech message	

ACTIVITIES

1 Call a radio station in your area and find out what the requirements are for getting a free-speech message on the air. Write a free-speech message, submit

it to a station, and make arrangements to record it in their studios. If the station does not accept your message, find out why it was rejected.

2 Visit a radio station and ask to see the public file. See if all the items listed in this chapter are included in the file. See if the file contains any citations issued by the FCC for violations. If so, see what measures the station had to take to rectify the situation.

The Station License

THE COMMERCIAL STATION LICENSE

There are many kinds of licenses issued by the Federal Communicatons Commission. You may have received a CB (citizens' band) license or perhaps even an amateur (shortwave) license. With either one of these two types you would be able to talk directly to another person by radio. This is called *direct address* or *point-to-point* communication and is illegal for the operator of a broadcasting station. *Broadcast* means that the messages sent are designed to be received by the general public rather than by a specific person, and for this reason the holder of a broadcast license must meet certain requirements and fulfill certain responsibilities.

When the FCC issues to you a radio broadcaster's license, you become the custodian of a valuable piece of public property. If you have a commercial license you are allowed to use your facilities to make a profit for the owners and stockholders, but you must also serve the *public interest*. The Commission is very clear on this point and stresses in several sections of *Rules and Regulations* that a broadcaster must operate in the "public interest, convenience and necessity." You may not go into the broadcasting business solely on the basis of speculation. For example, you are not permitted to sell the station for a profit until you have held the license at least 3 years. In addition, you are expected to devote a portion of your broadcast time to public service programs and spot announcements.

Making the Application

In order to receive a license for a commercial or noncommercial radio broadcasting station you must file application for a construction permit with the Federal Communications Commission. This is an application that says you have made an engineering study of the area where you wish the station to be located and have found a frequency within the broadcast band where your operation would not interfere with the transmission of any existing station. This part of the application requires extensive technical skills and equipment; it is a job usually performed by a consulting firm that specializes in this type of work. There are several criteria you have to meet.

   1 The application itself must be signed by a person who is qualified to become chief engineer of the station and who will give assurance that the licensee will operate the station within the required technical parameters.
   2 You have to reveal your financial resources and give evidence that you can afford to purchase the necessary equipment and maintain operation for a reasonable period of time.
   3 You have to meet all the legal qualifications of a licensee, such as being a citizen of the United States with no felony convictions.
   4 You have to give evidence that the community you wish to serve needs and desires the kind of programming you propose to offer. In other words you must show that the station will serve the "public interest, convenience, and necessity."

The last qualification is the most nebulous. How does one determine public interest, convenience, and necessity? In filing an application you would have to fill out form 301, section IV-A. Part one of this form reads as follows:

   A—State in Exhibit No._____the methods used by the applicant to ascertain the needs and interests of the public served by the station. Such information shall include (1) identification of representative groups, interests and organizations which were consulted, and (2) the major communities or areas which applicant principally undertakes to serve.

B—Describe in Exhibit No.____the significant needs and interests of the public which the applicant believes his station will serve during the coming license period, including those with respect to national and international matters.

C—List in Exhibit No.____typical and illustrative programs or program series (excluding Entertainment and News) that applicant plans to broadcast during the coming license period to meet those needs and interests.

The FCC does not expect that you will adhere to the stated programming schedule without change for the entire license period. However, when your license comes up for renewal, you will have to show what your program schedule was for a *composite week*. From that, the FCC will determine whether or not you have lived up to the spirit of your original application.

Ascertainment of Community Needs

In the past the section of the application regarding ascertainment of community needs had been treated rather lightly. But in recent years this has begun to change. There are not so many radio channels available as there used to be. In fact, in some areas there is no room for any more stations at all. Consequently there have been more *challenges* of licenses. When a license comes up for renewal, public notification must be made to that effect. Anyone wishing to complain about the performance of a station may do so. Furthermore, another party may challenge the owner's right to the license on grounds that a public service was not adequately performed. Licensees have therefore been forced to become more concerned about discovering community needs, and are making more conscientious surveys. In some cases even small stations have begun hiring *public affairs directors* to fulfill this responsibility. This, incidentally, might be a good opportunity for you to create a job opening for yourself. The first step would be to get hold of a copy of the *Ascertainment Primer* issued by the FCC in 1971.[1] It answers some of the questions regarding methods of ascertaining community problems, needs, and interests. You would have to contact community leaders and ask how your station can be of service. Colleges, for example, may wish to have courses broadcast over the air; law enforcement agencies may want to advise people how to protect themselves from crime; local government may desire that you generate an interest in political affairs; cultural organizations such as symphony orchestras and art galleries might want

[1] Frank J. Kahn, *Documents of American Broadcasting,* 2d ed. (Englewood Cliffs, N.J.: Prentice-Hall, 1973), pp. 316–325.

publicity about their activities. In making these inquiries you not only perform a public service, but also acquire ideas for new and interesting programs.

In addition to talking to community leaders, the FCC says a station must ascertain the needs of the general public. The survey must represent a proportional sample of the community. On this subject, the *Ascertainment Primer* states as follows:

> A professional service would not establish a dialogue between decision-making personnel in the applicant and community leaders. Therefore, such a service may not be used to consult community leaders. However, a professional service . . . may be used to conduct consultations with the general public. A professional service may also be used to provide the applicant with background data, including information as to the composition of the city of license. The use of a professional research or survey service is not required to meet Commission standards as to ascertaining community problems. The applicant will be responsible for the reliability of such a service.

Most commercial stations subscribe at some time to professional survey services. While they are considered accurate in determining the demographics of an audience and what they have been listening to, they can not be considered reliable predictors of what people *would* listen to if certain kinds of programs were offered. It may be necessary to experiment with programs to see how they are received. This is risky for a commercial station, and seldom are sweeping changes made in a program format that has been financially successful. It is more likely that stations will fulfill their obligations by inserting short programs or announcements into their regular format. Unfortunately these are often "buried" in the least desirable time periods.

Commercial Announcements

The FCC makes certain specific stipulations for the programming of commercial announcements. The most important rule is that all announcements for which a station is paid must contain clear sponsor identification. In other words, when the public is being persuaded, they have a right to know who is persuading them. Stations have received very stiff fines for failing to live up to this rule. It is the copywriter's job to see that the name of the sponsor is written into the commercial, and the traffic director's job to see that it appears in the log. Your job as combo operator would be to read the copy as written and log the time that you did so. Never read a commercial without logging it, and never log one without reading it.

There are questions that come up in regard to this rule. What about records that music distributors give to radio stations? The FCC does not require you to announce the name of the record company every time you play a song. This is considered to be a legitimate exchange in the broadcasting business as long as the station or the disk jockey does not receive any additional compensation for playing the record. Another exception would be the announcing of entertainment activities such as plays, concerts, and sporting events. This is all right to do in the context of news presented in the public interest. But again, the station or disk jockey must not receive any monetary compensation for doing this unless the announcement is logged and recorded as a commercial message. Sometimes a radio station will air an announcement that is referred to in the business as a *trade-out*. This means that the sponsor is not paying the station in cash, but is making facilities available to the station personnel. It is a common practice for stations to advertise resort hotels; instead of receiving money for the spot, the station manager or some members of the staff spend their vacation there. This is a legitimate practice as long as the sponsor is identified and the announcement is recorded and logged as a commercial. Most products can be advertised on broadcasting stations, but there are some exceptions. The most notable are cigarettes and hard liquor. The FCC says that commercial messages for these products are not in the public interest.

THE NONCOMMERCIAL STATION LICENSE

In addition to the general requirements discussed earlier in this chapter under "Making the Application," the FCC has specific rules for noncommercial license applicants (section 392 of the Communications Act). The most obvious, of course, is that there can be no commercial announcements. Although stations in this category can allow individuals to express opinions over the air, subject to the "equal time" clause, the licensee is not permitted to editorialize because noncommercial stations are largely financed by public funds.

Another rule pertains to colleges and universities seeking an educational broadcaster's license. The FCC will not issue such a license to a student organization. The license must be held by the board of trustees of the institution, even though students may be operating the station.

Twenty channels are made available by the FCC exclusively for the operation of noncommercial, educational FM broadcasting stations. Here is a table showing the channels available and their corresponding frequencies:

Frequency, MHz	Channel		Frequency, MHz	Channel
88.1	201		90.1	211
88.3	202		90.3	212
88.5	203		90.5	213
88.7	204		90.7	214
88.9	205		90.9	215
89.1	206		91.1	216
89.3	207		91.3	217
89.5	208		91.5	218
89.7	209		91.7	219
89.9	210		91.9	220

As you can see by the table the channels are numbered sequentially, while the frequencies increase by increments of 0.2 megahertz.[2] In actual practice the FCC would not assign directly adjacent channels to two stations in the same vicinity, because they would interfere with each other. You will also note that all the channels are at the lower end of the FM dial. The FM frequency band begins at 88 megahertz and goes to 108 megahertz.

PUBLIC SERVICE ANNOUNCEMENTS

All stations are required to devote a certain percentage of their time to public service announcements. The FCC does not make any rigid prescription as to the number or the content of such messages. Its description is as follows:

> A public service announcement is an announcement for which no charge is made and which promotes programs, activities or services of the Federal, State, or Local governments or the programs, activities or services of nonprofit organizations and other announcements regarded as serving the community interest. . . .[3]

The last phrase in this definition leaves broadcasters considerable latitude as to the type of public service announcements they may wish to log. Almost anything could be "regarded as serving the community inter-

[2] The term *megahertz* means "million cycles per second." The assigned frequencies of FM stations are expressed in this unit. The term was named after Heinrich Hertz, a nineteenth-century German scientist, who demonstrated the existence of the invisible electromagnetic waves now used in broadcasting. Megahertz is abbreviated MHz. The capital M is to distinguish it from the abbreviation for "milli," which uses a small m; capital H is used because it is the initial of a proper name.

[3] FCC *Rules and Regulations*, 73.112.

est." Most stations view public service announcements as an opportunity to provide valuable information to listeners about civic organizations and activities. While the definition appears to be vague, deciding the suitability of content for a public service announcement (PSA) presents no problem to most responsible broadcasters. Charitable organizations, such as the Goodwill Industries, Salvation Army, and United Crusade, qualify without question. Federal institutions, such as the military services and the National Safety Council, could be included. Local activities like the performance of a community orchestra would be seen as entitled to receive publicity through public service announcements. The fact that the work of an organization is controversial does not necessarily exclude it from falling under the heading of a public service. Planned Parenthood, for example, may not be endorsed by everyone, but it is a nonprofit organization and would qualify as a public service. Here the station must use some discretion, however. Announcements should not urge the use of contraceptives, but simply provide the information that the services of Planned Parenthood are available. Causes may be espoused, but only when they are clearly in the interest of the entire population. You can urge people to vote, to fasten their safety belts, to stop smoking, to use less energy, and to refrain from littering—but not to join a union, buy more peanut butter, or write to a congressman about a specific piece of legislation. The broadcaster is expected to use good judgment in determining what is or is not a public service announcement.

RENEWING A STATION LICENSE

All broadcasting stations, both commercial and noncommercial, must renew their licenses every 3 years. At this time the FCC looks very closely at both the technical performance and the programming of the station. The engineering staff is required to provide a *proof of performance* that demonstrates that the station has been operating and will continue to operate within the required technical tolerances of its license. The programming staff must submit a *composite week* of program logs, consisting of 7 days from the preceding 3-year period. (The days are chosen by the FCC, not by the station.) From this composite week, the FCC will make a determination as to whether or not the station has been fulfilling its obligations. For noncommercial stations, the Commission looks at five different program types, which are described in section IV of FCC form 342 as follows:

> *Instructional* (I) includes all programs designed to be utilized with facilities of educational institutions in the regular instructional program of the

institution. In-school, in-service for teachers, and "extension" courses for academic credit are examples of instructional programs.

General educational (GEN) is an educational program for which no formal credit is given.

Performing arts (A) is a program such as drama, concert, opera, or dance (live or recorded), in which the performing aspect predominates.

Public affairs (PA) includes talks, discussions, speeches, documentaries, editorials, forums, panels, round tables, and similar programs primarily concerning local, national, and international affairs or problems.

Light entertainment (E) includes casually diverting programs of popular music or talk.

Other (O) includes all programs not falling within the definitions of instructional, general education, performing arts, public affairs, or light entertainment. Such programs as news or sports should be reported as "other."

In the license renewal application, the FCC wants to know the total number of hours and the percentage of time devoted to these program types in the composite week. The form looks like this:

State for a full week submitted in 1(a) above the amount of time devoted to the following types of programs (totals to equal 100%)

	Type of Program	Hours	Percentage
1.	Instructional		
2.	General Educational		
3.	Performing Arts		
4.	Public Affairs		
5.	Light Entertainment		
6.	Other		
	Total		100%

The FCC does not specify how much time should be spent on each type, but broadcasters are generally expected to program something other than just light entertainment.

SUMMARY

In order to obtain a broadcasting license, an applicant must be able to demonstrate an ability to serve the "public interest, convenience, and necessity." To receive a license for a radio station you must file a Construction Permit with the Federal Communications Commission showing that there is a frequency available in the area you wish to serve. You must ascertain the needs of the community and then be willing to offer programs that meet those needs. As the license holder of a commercial station you are permitted to make a profit, but you must also provide a public service. In renewing your license every three years, you will have to be prepared to show that you are meeting your responsibilities in maintaining technical requirements in your transmission and that your programming meets the needs of the public.

TERMINOLOGY

Ascertainment
Ascertainment Primer
Channel
Composite week
Construction permit
Direct address

Megahertz
Proof of performance
Public interest
Public service announcement
  (PSA)
Trade-out

ACTIVITIES

1 Write to the Federal Communications Commission, and ask them to send you the forms for a construction permit for a noncommercial station. Get acquainted with the paperwork that must be filed to start a station. Look in your school or public library for the Communications Act of 1934. Find section 392 and become familiar with the application for a grant to construct a noncommercial broadcasting station. Find out how many noncommercial stations operate in your area. See if you can find a channel that might still be available.

2 Make a list of organizations that run public service announcements on the radio. Listen to several stations and jot down the names of the organizations when you hear the announcements. Add to the list organizations and causes that you would include if you owned a station.

Chapter 5

The Operator's Permit

THE NEED FOR A PERMIT

Talking on the radio does not require a permit—anyone can do that. But the operator of broadcasting equipment must have one, just as the operator of a motor vehicle must have a license. If you control technical functions of a station, by turning on the transmitter or regulating the volume of sound that will be broadcast, the Federal Communications Commission says that you must hold the proper license or permit. Recently the FCC has modified its requirements for broadcast operators. Under the new regulations, all that is required is a *Restricted Radiotelephone Operator Permit,* which can be obtained by any United States citizen simply by filing an application. You can acquire the necessary form at any FCC office. With this permit you would be authorized to operate any FM station and most of the lower-powered AM stations. To operate the higher-powered AM stations or those with directional antenna arrays, you would need a Radiotelephone Operator License First

Class. This license qualifies you to operate any broadcasting station, and it is valuable to anyone pursuing a broadcasting career. However, it is very difficult to obtain a license. To pass the test requires many weeks or months of intensive study and probably a course oriented to this aspect of electronics. Having a first class license (commonly referred to as a "first phone") is an indication that you are serious about the profession, and it increases your job opportunities.

The change in license requirements for broadcast operators was made by the FCC in the early part of 1979. Prior to that time all operators had to hold at least a *Radiotelephone Third Class* Operator Permit. Even though that is no longer a requirement of the FCC, some stations maintain the policy of having their operators hold the permit.

OBTAINING THE PERMIT

To obtain the third class operator's permit you must pass two tests called *Elements*. Element One deals with basic law; Element Two deals with basic operating practices. Each test contains twenty questions and you must score 75 percent on each to pass. The tests are given only on certain

Figure 5-1 Radiotelephone Third Class operator permit. *(Photo by Wayne Fogle.)*

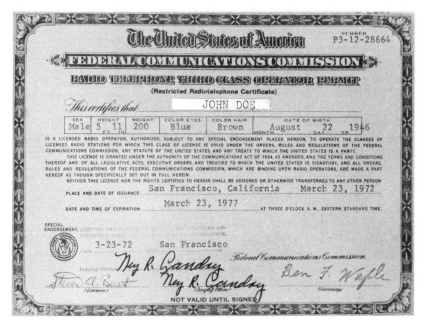

days and at certain times. You can find out where and when the tests are given at the FCC office in your area. You may wish to obtain a copy of the FCC *Broadcast Operator Handbook* to prepare for the tests.[1] This can be found at offices of the FCC or any government bookstore. You can get other manuals on the subject from the library or from electronics stores. A suggested list is offered in the bibliography of this text.

DEFINITIONS

One of the first things you must do to prepare for the FCC examinations is to learn the terminology. The FCC uses terms in a way that may not be familiar to you, and it is necessary for you to learn their definitions. The following is a list of commonly used terms and the definitions provided by the FCC.

Broadcast day   That period of time between local sunrise and 12 midnight local time. (*Rules and Regulations,* 73.9)

Daytime   That period of time between local sunrise and local sunset. (*Rules and Regulations,* 73.6)

FM broadcast station   A broadcast station transmitting frequency modulated radiotelephone (voice type) emissions primarily intended to be received by the general public, and operated on a channel in the 88- to 108-MHz band. (*Rules and Regulations,* 73.310)

FM stereophonic broadcast   The transmission of a stereophonic program by an FM broadcast station utilizing the main channel and a stereophonic sub-channel. (*Rules and Regulations,* 73.310)

FM Subsidiary Communications Authorization (SCA)   An authorization granted to an FM station for the simultaneous transmission of one or more signals on assigned subcarrier frequencies within the station's assigned channel. Special decoding equipment is required to receive program material furnished on the SCA subchannel. Such material, although broadcast related, is normally intended for paying subscribers. (*Rules and Regulations,* 73.293)

Nighttime   That period of time between local sunset and local sunrise. (*Rules and Regulations,* 73.7)

Nominal power   The power of a standard broadcast station as specified in a system of classification which includes the following values: 50 kW, 25 kW, 10 kW, 5 kW, 1 kW, 0.5 kW, 0.25 kW. (*Rules and Regulations,* 73.14)

Standard broadcast (AM) station   A broadcast station transmitting amplitude modulated (voice type) emissions primarily intended to be received by the general public, and operated on a frequency in the 535- to 1,605-kHz band. (*Rules and Regulations,* 73.1)

Sunrise and sunset   For each particular location and during any particular month, the times of sunrise and sunset are specified on most AM broadcast

---

[1] *Broadcast Operator Handbook: Radiotelephone 3rd Class Operator Permit,* U.S. Government Printing Office, Washington, 1976.

station licenses. This is necessary because not all standard (AM) broadcast stations are permitted to operate at night. In order to control objectionable skywave interference, stations which are permitted to operate at night are frequently required to change their modes of operation. These changes may involve the use of directional antenna systems, a reduction in operating power, or both, and normally occur at the sunrise and sunset times listed in the station license. (*Rules and Regulations,* 73.8)

BASIC LAW

The Federal Communications Commission was created by the Communications Act of 1934 for the purpose of regulating interstate and foreign commerce in communication by radio and wire. Among the powers given to the Commission is the authority to prescribe the qualifications of station operators, to classify them according to the duties they are to perform, and to issue commercial operator's licenses to United States citizens.

Obtaining New Licenses

To obtain a commercial Radiotelephone Third Class Operator Permit, an applicant must first submit the appropriate application forms at a convenient FCC field office. If the applicant passes the examination and there are no doubts as to his or her nationality, character, or physical condition, a license will be routinely issued. There are no age, experience, or educational requirements.

Term of License Renewal

An operator's license is normally issued for a 5-year term and may be renewed during the last year. An operator who files an application for renewal before the expiration date may post a copy of the application where the license was posted and continue to operate even though the renewed license may not arrive until after the expiration date of the old license. An operator's license may also be renewed without reexamination during a one-year grace period following its expiration date. The license is not valid during this period and the operator must wait until the renewed license is issued before resuming operation of a station. Operators who file for renewal after the one-year grace period must be reexamined before they can obtain new licenses.

Duplicate and Replacement Licenses

Should an operator's license become lost, mutilated, or destroyed, or if the operator's name has been changed, a duplicate or replacement license may be requested by filing an application with the Commission field office which issued the original license. If the old license is available, it must accompany the application for a duplicate or replacement; if it is found later, it must be returned to the Commission for cancellation.

Posting Operator Licenses

Most third class operator's permits are required to be posted at the operator's place of duty. When an application for a duplicate, replacement, or renewal of a commercial operator license is submitted, the license then held, if available, must accompany the application. In this case the operator may post a signed copy of the submitted application in lieu of the license document.

Cancelling Operator Licenses

If the holder of a lower-class license qualifies for a higher-class license, the lower-class license will be cancelled upon issuance of the new license.

Failing an Examination Element

An applicant who fails a commercial operator's examination element will be ineligible to retake that same element for a 2-month period.

Official Notice of Violation

Operators are expected to abide by the Commission's rules governing the station they are operating. An operator who violates these rules may be served with a written notice pointing out the violations and requesting a statement concerning the matter. FCC form 793 may be used for this purpose. Within 10 days from receipt of such notice, the operator must send a written reply to the office of the Commission originating the official notice.

Suspension of Operator Licenses

The Commission has the authority to suspend the license of any operator who has:

    1 Violated any provision of any act, treaty, or convention binding on the United States which the Commission is authorized to administer, or any regulation made by the Commission under any such act, treaty, or convention;

    2 failed to carry out a lawful order of the master or person lawfully in charge of the ship or aircraft on which he [or she] is employed;

    3 willfully damaged or permitted radio apparatus or installations to be damaged;

   4 transmitted superfluous radio communications or signals or communications containing profane or obscene words, language, or meaning;

   5 knowingly transmitted false or deceptive communications;

   6 knowingly transmitted a call signal or letter which has not been assigned by proper authority to the station [he or she] is operating

   7 willfully or maliciously interfered with any other radio communications or signals;

   8 obtained or attempted to obtain, or has assisted another to obtain, an operator's license by fraudulent means.[2]

An order of suspension will be in writing and will take effect 15 days after it is received. During those 15 days, the operator may apply to the Commission for a hearing on the order of suspension. Upon receipt of such application the order will be held in abeyance until the conclusion of the hearing, at which time the Commission may

affirm the order of suspension which becomes effective immediately
modify the order of suspension, *or*
cancel the order

Inspection of Radio Stations

Representatives of the Commission have the authority to inspect all radio installations, associated with stations required to be licensed, at any reasonable hour; this includes nights and weekends. The purpose of an inspection is to ascertain whether in construction, installation, and operation the station conforms to the requirements of the rules and regulations governing radio communications.

BASIC THEORY

There is no need for you to have a background in electronics to operate broadcasting equipment. But you will find it valuable to have some knowledge of the concepts and the terminology so you will know what you are doing. Radio transmission is effected by electromagnetic waves which move through the air in a fashion similar to waves that move through water. Just as a pebble creates a disturbance on the surface of a pond, so a radio transmitter creates a disturbance in the air. The wave that is produced looks like that shown in Figure 5-2. Such a wave is called a *sine wave,* and the figure shows the alternations of the wave from positive to negative. Each complete alternation is called one *cycle.* The number of cycles that occur in each second is called the *frequency.* The distance from the base line to the high or low point of the wave is called

[2] Communications Act of 1934, section 303 (m).

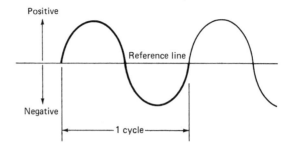

Figure 5-2 Sine wave.

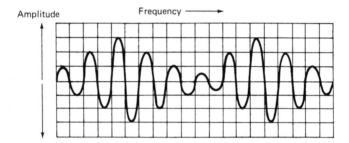

Figure 5-3 Amplitude modulation.

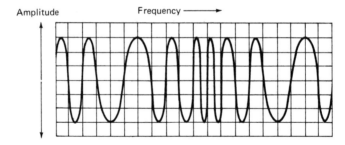

Figure 5-4 Frequency modulation.

the *amplitude.* Think of these waves as being vibrations, some of which produce sound that we can hear, and others that are above our range. The human ear cannot pick up tones beyond about 20,000 cycles per second, and this frequency is generally taken as the upper limit of the audio range. Radio frequencies, on the other hand, are measured in the hundreds of thousands or millions of cycles per second.

A radio transmitter will operate on an assigned *carrier frequency.* That is to say, the FCC will assign to a station a particular broadcasting channel on the AM or FM band. Let's say a station has been given the frequency of 1,400 kilohertz on the AM band. That means the *signal* (radio wave) is oscillating (producing alternations) at 1,400 thousand cycles per second. Radio frequencies, of course, are far above the range of human hearing, so these vibrations are not audible. The radio frequency carries or transports the audible sound (originating in the studio) that has been translated into electric impulses. At the receiving end a radio tuner can be adjusted to the desired channel and the audible frequency separated from the radio frequency.

The sound that is transported by the carrier frequency is called the *modulation.* Modulation simply means change. We are changing the radio frequency carrier by combining it electrically with the audio (program) frequencies. We can effect those changes either by modulating the *amplitude* or the *frequency* of the carrier. This is the difference between AM (amplitude modulation) and FM (frequency modulation) radio. (See Figures 5-3 and 5-4.)

READING METERS

One of the responsibilities you will have as the operator of a broadcasting station is to read the meters of the transmission equipment and log the readings every three hours. In order to understand what you are doing, you need to know the basic principles. Here are some of the terms and definitions:

Current This is the flow of electricity. Think of it as water flowing through a pipe. It is measured in *amperes,* commonly called "amps".

Voltage This is the force that pushes the current. Think of it as the pump that pushes water through the pipe. It is measured in *volts.*

Resistance This is the load that is put upon the flow of electricity. Think of it as the paddle that is turned by the flow of water. It is measured in *ohms.*

Power This is the rate at which work is done. Think of a paddle wheel delivering energy to its shaft. Electrical power is measured in *watts.*

Modulation This means change from high to low. Think of it as the vibrations that produce sound. When you play a record or a tape or talk into a microphone, you are causing modulation. Figure 5-8 shows a modulation meter.

Carrier frequency The radio signal which is transmitted through the air and which carries audible sound.

Sine wave This is an electrical wave consisting of alternations from positive to negative. Think of it as the cross section of a wave in the water.

Amplitude The distance between the base line of a sine wave and the high or low point of the wave.

Cycles per second The number of alternations that occur in a sine wave every second. Measured in *hertz*.

Kilo This is a prefix that means "thousand." It is frequently found before the word "watt." One kilowatt is equal to one thousand watts.

Mega This is a prefix that means "million." One megahertz is the same as one million cycles per second.

Milli This is a prefix that means "one thousandth." One milliamp is equal to one 1,000th of an ampere. It would be written as 0.001 amp.

Using these definitions, you can begin to understand how to read meters. Be sure to remember the following important considerations:

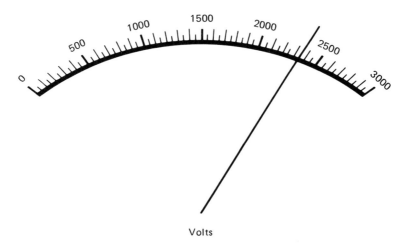

Figure 5-5 Voltmeter. The reading is 2,350 volts. It could also be read as 2.35 kilovolts.

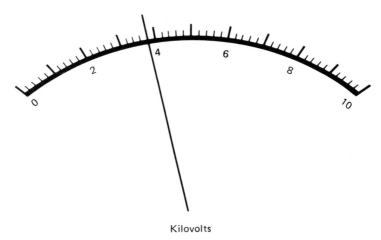

Figure 5-6 Kilovoltmeter. The reading is 3.8. It could also be read as 3,800 volts.

1 Note how the meter is *labeled.* A *wattmeter* will give you a different reading from a *kilowattmeter.*

2 Note the graduations between the numbers. You have to be able to see well enough to count the marks between the numerical values.

3 Know what the meter is supposed to read. This information will be given to you by the chief engineer. A corrective adjustment may be made *after* the reading has been logged. Figure 5-5 shows a meter that registers volts.

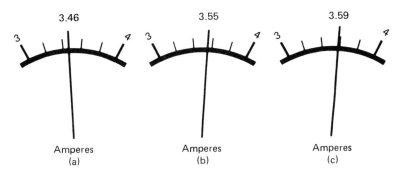

Figure 5-7 Ammeters. These ammeters are registering the current going to three separate antennas. Note how the meters are read when all the graduations are not marked on the scale.

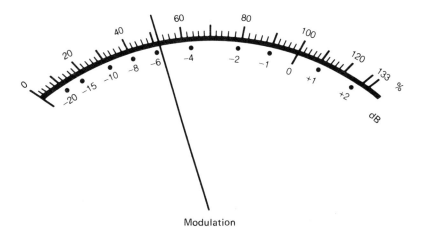

Figure 5-8 Modulation meter. This meter indicates the average level of modulation. The percent scale at the top is the one to read. The decibel scale at the bottom can be disregarded. The meter reads 52 percent modulation.

DIRECTIONAL AM STATIONS

One of the important functions of the Federal Communications Commission is to maximize broadcasting service to the public. If two stations are on adjacent frequencies and located close to each other geographically, there is danger of one signal overlapping the other. This is particularly true after sundown, because radio transmission carries farther at night than it does in the daytime. To prevent broadcast signals from interfering with one another the FCC issues licenses with several kinds of special provisions. One might be that the station be permitted to operate only from sunrise to sunset. A station of this type is called a "daytimer." Another provision might be that a station would have to reduce its power at night; another, that the station would be licensed to operate with a *directional antenna* array (see Figure 5-9).

A station which is required to control the radiation of its signal in some directions must use a directional antenna system consisting of antennas mounted on two or more towers. With this type of system the radio signal can be "aimed" in the desired directions so that adjacent stations are protected.

Because of the complex nature of directional transmission, the FCC requires that an operator in these stations have a Radiotelephone Operator License First Class. Directional stations are usually a thousand watts or more and located in the larger metropolitan areas. For these reasons they can generally afford to pay higher salaries—a fact that may motivate you to get a "first phone."

STEREO AND SCA

In monophonic broadcasting only one audio signal is transmitted and it requires only one speaker for true reproduction. Television and AM radio are examples of monophonic broadcasting. In stereophonic broadcasting two audio signals are combined and transmitted over a single channel in such a way that a listener with a stereo receiver can separate the two signals for reproduction through separate speakers. The reason for using two signals is to afford the listener a sense of the spatial distribution of the original sound sources. The stereo signal may also be received and reproduced through a monophonic system; in that case, however, the spatial distribution effect will be lost.

In addition to monaural (monophonic) operation, an FM station may, without further authority, broadcast stereo programming provided

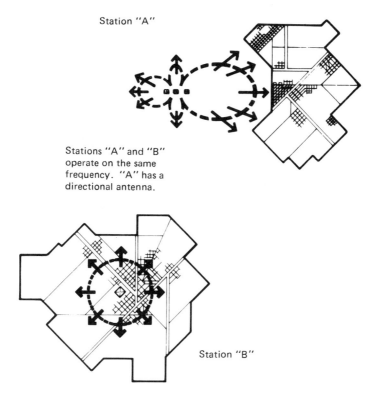

Station "A"

Stations "A" and "B" operate on the same frequency. "A" has a directional antenna.

Station "B"

Figure 5-9 Directional antenna array. Station B is protected by the directional pattern of station A.

its modulation monitor is approved for stereophonic operation. There are no additional logging or monitoring requirements.

An FM station may also transmit signals other than stereo within its assigned channel, but for this it requires a Subsidiary Communications Authorization (SCA). Programs transmitted under authority of an SCA cannot be received without a special receiver or adaptor.

SCA programs are used mainly for subscription background music but may also carry detailed weather forecasting, special time signals, or other material of a broadcast nature intended for business, professional, educational, religious, trade, labor, agriculture, or other special interest groups. The operator must monitor and control SCA programming.

Station identification announcements need not be made on SCA programs; however, each licensee must maintain an SCA program log in which a general description of the material transmitted is entered daily.

In order to develop the proper signal, stations transmitting SCA programming employ special modulation techniques using "subcarriers." An operating log must be maintained for the SCA subchannel.[3]

EMERGENCY BROADCAST SYSTEM

The Emergency Broadcast System (EBS) was developed for the purpose of providing the President of the United States and the heads of state and local governments with a means of communicating with the general public in the event of a major or widespread emergency. The National EBS can be activated only on orders from the President. The activation notification would be sent to the major radio and television networks, the American Telephone and Telegraph Company, The Associated Press, and United Press International. From these points the notification would be disseminated throughout the country by teletype and broadcast.

All broadcasting stations must be equipped with an EBS monitor. It will be tuned to a key station that has been designated as a receiver of the notification. The key station will activate your monitor by shutting off its own transmitter. When it comes back on ten seconds later it will broadcast instructions that you will be able to hear on your monitor. You have probably heard the system tested on your local station. Usually the announcer comes on after a tone and says, "This has been a test of the Emergency Broadcast System." If there were a national emergency, you would hear instructions rather than the announcement of a test. Each individual station has its own role to play in the Emergency Broadcast System. When you go to work for a broadcasting station, be sure to find out from the chief engineer what the special instructions are for your station.

MALFUNCTIONS

As the operator of a broadcasting station you are responsible for its technical performance. Malfunctions are bound to occur—some more serious than others—and you must know what action to take.

The FCC says that whenever the transmitting system is observed operating (1) beyond the posted parameters, or (2) in any other manner inconsistent with the rules, or (3) in any other manner inconsistent with the terms of the station license; and the adjustments a third class operator is permitted to make cannot correct the condition . . . the transmitter must be turned off. (Major adjustments to the transmission equipment

---

[3] Ibid., p. 69.

can only be made by the holder of a first class operator's license.) An example of this kind of major malfunction would be an increase in the station's power beyond its designated parameter, or an excessive deviation from the assigned frequency.

Here are some other, less serious malfunctions.

Modulation monitor fails Continue operating; notify the station licensee, who will arrange for alternate means of monitoring.

Underpower Continue operating; notify the station licensee. (This could happen at sunrise when the operator is unable to increase power to daytime conditions.)

EBS monitor fails Notify the station licensee; monitor using another radio receiver if available.

Tower lighting failure If any top light or flashing beacon fails, notify the FAA (Federal Aviation Administration). If failure is in the side lights, make an entry in the operating log.

For other types of malfunctions, check with the chief engineer at your station.

Remember that you may be visited by an inspector from the FCC while you are on duty at a broadcasting station. Be sure your own license or permit is displayed as required; that you can point to the station license; that you know where the station's public file is located; that your EBS monitor is operating, and you know what to do if it is activated; and that you can get in touch with the chief engineer.

SUMMARY

You need a license or permit only if you are the operator of a broadcasting station and have control of the essential equipment that regulates transmission. New regulations require only that you have a *restricted permit* for the operation of most broadcasting stations. A third class license is still required by many station owners, and a first class license is highly desirable for people who want to advance their careers in radio. AM stations with directional antenna arrays require the "first phone." As the operator of the station you will need to know how to take meter readings and have some understanding of the terminology. You should be familiar with the Subsidiary Communications Authorization if you plan to work in a commercial FM station that operates in stereo. You also need to know about the Emergency Broadcast System and what to do in case of malfunctions. It is important for your own sake and that of the station that you be prepared to answer the questions of an FCC inspector.

TERMINOLOGY

Amplitude   Milli
Carrier frequency   Modulation
Current   Power
Emergency Broadcast System   Radiotelephone
   System (EBS)   Resistance
First phone   Sine wave
Frequency   Standard broadcast
Kilo   Voltage
Mega

ACTIVITIES

1 Write or call the Federal Communications Commission and request an application for a restricted permit. Fill it out and send it in.
2 Get the *Broadcast Operator Handbook* from the library, a bookshop, or electronics store. Read up on the requirements for obtaining the Radiotelephone Third Class Operator Permit. Find out from the office of the FCC when the tests are given for Elements One and Two.
3 Call a local radio station and find out what license or permit is required.
4 Study the material in the license handbook; then take the tests for the third class permit.

Operating the Equipment

THE BASIC EQUIPMENT

The best opportunity for the beginner in broadcasting will be as a *combo operator*. To be eligible you must have a license or a permit and be able to operate the equipment effectively. You will work in a studio called *master control*. This is normally a small room with just enough space for the operator and the *audio equipment*. The audio equipment consists of a console, turntables, tape recorders, microphones, and possibly a patch panel. You will be seated in the middle of a "U" shaped configuration with all of the equipment within easy reach. In the beginning you will find operation of the equipment difficult and perhaps confusing, but you will learn to work with it just as you were able to learn to drive a car. Eventually the physical operation will become second nature, and you will be able to give full attention to what you are saying without having to think about which button you are going to push.

You may be acquainted with much of the equipment already. Turntables, tape recorders, and microphones are common appliances in many homes. If you own hi-fi equipment you are perhaps already familiar with the fundamentals of studio operation. Professional broadcast "gear" may be different in several respects, however, and it is those differences that we are going to discuss in this chapter. One basic difference is that professional equipment is usually *low impedance* while your home equipment is probably *high impedance*. Impedance is the electrical property that one piece of equipment "presents," as *load* or as *source,* to another piece of equipment to which it is connected. The high-impedance microphone, for example, that you use with your home tape recorder would not be compatible with the low-impedance input circuit of a professional tape recorder. In fact, even the connecting plug would probably not match. Let us look closely at each piece of equipment, examine its function, and see how it works. Understand, of course, that the explanations and descriptions that are offered here are only preliminary. You will only become familiar with the equipment by getting actual "hands-on" experience. After reading this chapter, you will want to sit down in front of an *audio console* and see for yourself where the switches and knobs are located. You will note that everything is connected to this basic piece of equipment. The volume for the microphones, turntables and tape recorders are all controlled by knobs that are called "pots"—short for *potentiometer*—mounted on the console. There will also be switches that will turn on or off the signal coming from each unit. Figure 6-1 shows a master control room.

MICROPHONES

The first unit we want to consider is a tool that is as fundamental to an announcer as a hammer is to a carpenter—the microphone. For many people it is a fearful instrument, but as a professional you must understand it and be comfortable using it. There are many different types and styles of microphones: They differ in quality, construction, and performance. You can purchase some microphones for under five dollars; others cost several hundred. The common function of all of them is to produce tiny voltages which vary according to the sound waves that impinge on their moving elements. In terms of construction, there are three different types:

1 In a *ribbon* or *velocity* microphone the moving element is a thin, metallic ribbon, vibrating within a magnetic field.
2 In a *dynamic* or *pressure* microphone a wire coil attached to a diaphragm vibrates in a magnetic field.

Figure 6-1 Master Control. *(Courtesy KMEL.)*

3 In a *condenser* microphone the plates of a condenser constitute the vibrating mechanism.

The differences in sound quality produced by the three systems are very subtle. You may want to experiment with all three to see which one sounds best with your voice. The most widely used is the dynamic mike. It is versatile and more durable than the other two. Ribbon and condenser microphones are very sensitive and sometimes more flattering to the voice, but they do not sound well out-of-doors or when the performer is working too close. But these differences are relatively minor. The most significant distinctions to be made among microphones have to do with their directions of sensitivity—their so-called "pickup patterns." There are three major patterns, with an infinite number of gradations from one to another.

Omnidirectional

An omnidirectional (or "nondirectional") microphone (Figure 6-2) is one that picks up from all directions. It is good for recording several different voices as you would have in a group discussion. But it picks up noises in the background too. The more people you have around one microphone the farther away they have to be, and the more you have to turn up the

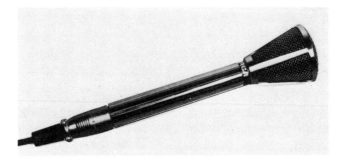

Figure 6-2 Omnidirectional microphone. Model BK-14. *(Courtesy RCA.)*

volume. As you increase the gain (volume) you also increase the ambient sounds. But if you have only one microphone and want to pick up several voices, the omnidirectional mike is the kind to use because it does not have to be aimed every time a different person speaks.

Unidirectional

A unidirectional (or "directional") microphone (Figure 6-3) picks up sound mainly from one direction, suppressing the sounds from the back. The most commonly used unidirectional mike has a *cardioid* (heart-shaped) pattern. The announcer can talk in the 180-degree radius of the mike's effective range, but sounds coming from behind the microphone

Figure 6-3 Unidirectional microphone. Model BK-5. *(Courtesy RCA.)*

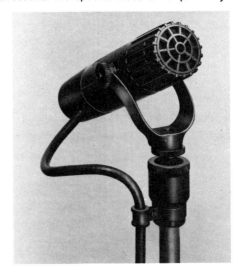

will hardly be heard. This mike is widely used in master control where normally only one person is talking into it.

Bidirectional

A bidirectional microphone (Figure 6-4) is "live" on the front and back but suppresses sound on the top and sides. It is a useful mike in a studio where two people are talking face to face. It minimizes the ambient sounds but allows more than just one person to talk while maintaining good quality reproduction. It is possible, for example, to have a loud-speaker (monitor) turned up with a bidirectional mike and not get feed-back noise—provided the speaker is on a dead side of the mike.

Hand-held Mikes

A considerable portion of modern broadcasting involves interviews. Much of this work is done outside the studio with portable equipment. When two people have to talk to each other on one directional mike, it might have to be hand-held and moved from one person to another.

Figure 6-4 Bidirectional microphone. Model 77 DX. *(Courtesy RCA.)*

Figure 6-5 Hand-held microphone. Model BK 16. *(Courtesy RCA.)*

Only a mike designed for this purpose should be used (see Figure 6-5). An inexpensive microphone will rattle and produce distracting noises when any portion of it is touched even lightly. Usually a microphone used in this way will be equipped with a *windscreen*—a plastic foam sleeve that will filter out some of the noise created by wind and other disturbances. When conducting an interview with a hand-held mike there is one important rule to remember. *Hold the microphone yourself.* Do not give it to the person to whom you are talking. If you do, you will lose control of the interview. An overly loquacious individual may not have the sense of timing that you, as a professional, should have. He or she may talk too long, and you might have trouble getting the micro- phone back. Holding the mike yourself allows you to get your own com- ments in, and also makes it possible for you to give the other person direct "cues" so he knows when to talk.

Clip-on Mikes

You may also find it useful to attach a microphone to the person who is talking. The advantage of a clip-on microphone (Figure 6-6) is that it will stay with you and still give you use of your hands if you have to move around. It is inconspicuous and often less threatening to a novice who may have anxieties about talking into a microphone. A variation is a *lavalier* microphone which can be hung around a person's neck. These types of microphones are more commonly used in television, but radio stations find them useful also.

Microphones are very sensitive. They will record and transmit all the sounds they hear—even the ones you may not want them to hear. Never mumble under your breath or whisper to the person next to you.

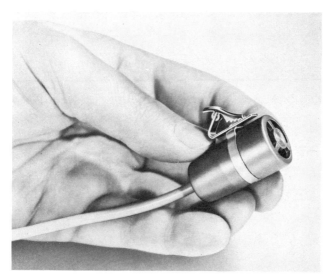

Figure 6-6 Clip-on microphone. Model BK 12. *(Courtesy RCA.)*

The mike will pick up all subverbal sounds and inaudible words. The audience will react the same way anyone else does when someone whispers in their presence. They will feel left out.

Checking the Mike

Before you go on the air the microphone must be set at the appropriate volume level. This will be done by the engineer, or by you yourself if you are serving as your own engineer. It is done with the aid of a *volume unit meter*—commonly referred to as a *VU meter* (Figure 6-7). When you talk into the microphone the needle of the meter should *peak at 100 percent modulation.* That is the point on the meter just before the shaded area; it is also called *zero level.* Up to that point on the meter you are getting true reproduction of sound. When the needle goes beyond that point—into the red or dark-shaded area you are only adding distortion. To check the microphone, switch it on, turn up the volume, and talk into the microphone. The needle will begin to bounce. The volume should be set so that the apex of the bounce is at the start of the red-shaded area on the meter. When you are checking the microphone, speak at the volume you will use when you go on the air, and place yourself in the position you intend to work from. Keep talking until you get a satisfactory reading. If you make just one sound, the needle will bounce up and back and you will not be able to make the necessary adjustments. You can recite some-

Figure 6-7 Volume unit meter. *(Courtesy RCA.)*

thing, ad lib, or read copy—it doesn't matter what you say. But do not tap the microphone or blow into it. That is bad for the microphone and does not allow you to set the level.

TURNTABLES

There will be at least two turntables in every control room, sometimes three. Each will have an on-off switch and a speed control. Professional turntables start very fast and are designed to reach full speed almost instantaneously. (See Figure 6-8.)

Cuing a Record

Good broadcasting practice requires that you keep your operation *tight*. That is, you do not want *dead air* at any time. Even a few seconds of silence is too much. This means that you have to take up the slack that exists between the time the needle is placed at the start of the groove on the record and the time the music actually begins. This is called *cuing the record.*

Figure 6-8 Turntable. Model GT3-12. *(Courtesy Cetec Broadcast Group.)*

First you switch on the "cuing amplifier" which will allow you to hear the record without the sound being broadcast. Then put the needle in the groove and turn on the turntable. Stop it when the first sound of the music is heard and back the record off half a turn. The record is now "cued." When you are ready to play it, it will start instantaneously.

Segue

When one record ends, you must do something right away to avoid dead air. You may want to open your microphone and talk, but if you have nothing to say you can *segue* (pronounced SEG-way) right into the next record. That means starting the second one just as the first one ends. Sometimes the policy of a station is to segue two or three records in a row and then *back-announce* the entire *set*. Obviously, this is done more frequently on stations that are not heavy with commercials. (See Figure 6-9.)

Cross Fade

A cross fade is similar to a segue except that you do not wait for the first record to end. You start the second record's turntable with its volume control turned down while the first is still playing. You then turn down the volume on the first while turning up the volume on the second. This must be done skillfully, because there is a point in the transition when both records are heard simultaneously. If they are not in harmony, the sound will be cacophonous. (See Figure 6-9.)

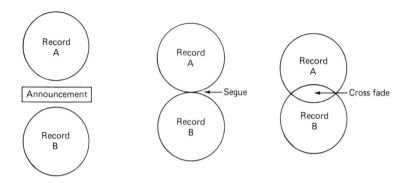

Figure 6-9 Cross fade and segue.

Music Under

Sometimes you may want to talk while the music is "under" you. There are two choices: You can start the record at full volume; then turn it down, open your mike and begin talking. Or, you can start talking first; then "sneak" the music in under you. In either case be sure that your voice predominates over the music; otherwise what you say will be lost. And never talk over a vocal; always use an instrumental selection. Sometimes the term "voice-over" is used instead of "music under."

Back-timing

In some cases it may be necessary to end a program on the exact second. For example, you may have to join a network program that starts on the hour. It is very difficult to anticipate precisely when your record will end. If it goes long you will have to fade it out (turn the volume down), which you may not want to do. An alternative is to *back-time* the record. Pick a record that has been timed either by the manufacturer or by your station. Let's say it runs 2 minutes and 38 seconds. At exactly that length of time before the hour, you start the turntable with the volume control turned down. Then, when your first record ends, you can talk, close out your program, and as you do, sneak in the back-timed record. It will end exactly on the hour.

TAPE EQUIPMENT

Master control will also be equipped with two reel-to-reel tape recorders (see Figure 6-10). One is not enough because you may have to come out of one tape-recorded program and go directly into another. The term "reel-to-reel" is used to distinguish this kind of equipment from cartridge or cassette machines. Cartridges will be discussed later; cassettes are hardly ever used directly in broadcast. Most people have seen home tape recorders and are familiar with them. Professional machines used in broadcasting are basically similar but incorporate certain refinements.

Speed Control

Tape recorder speeds are measured in *inches per second* (ips). Some home machines will record as slow as 1⅞ ips, but a professional broadcast

Figure 6-10   Reel-to-reel tape recorder. Model ATR-700. *(Courtesy Ampex Corporation.)*

recorder would not be able to play it back. Next is 3¾ ips. This is all right to use for long-talk-type programs. It uses up tape at a slower rate, but the fidelity is not as good as it is at the faster speeds. The standard speed for most broadcast tapes is 7½ ips. At this speed the fidelity will be good, and a 7-inch reel of tape will last 30 minutes. (At 3¾ ips it will last a full hour.) Some professional machines will play at 15 ips, but this uses up tape very fast, and the improved fidelity is unimportant in most cases.

Direction Controls

All reel-to-reel tape recorders have controls that include *play, stop, fast forward, rewind,* and *record.* In conjunction with these may be a *counter* which advances in number as the tape moves forward. These are useful in locating portions of your program, but you must remember to set the counter on zero when you start. Incidentally, counter readings are usually arbitrary numbers, not minutes and seconds; so they probably will not coincide from one machine to another. The controls on a tape recorder are easy enough to operate. Your tape is erased automatically when you push *record.* The manufacturer protects you from erasing something accidentally by having you push two buttons instead of just one to put the machine into the record mode.

Record and Play Indicators

Better-quality recorders will be equipped with VU meters or other indicators to enable the operator to set record and play *levels.* The volume level should be set before you begin to record. To set the level, put the machine in record mode; then talk into the microphone as described earlier. Some recorders will have an "in-out" switch. Set this switch in the *record,* or *source* position, and set your levels for recording, but move the switch back to *play* when you want to play back.

Input and Output Jacks

On one side of the tape recorder will be the *input* and *output* jacks.[1] Their names describe exactly what they do. One input jack will be for the microphone (you are putting your voice *in*). Another jack may say *line in.* This would be used if you want to record something directly from a phonograph, radio, or another tape recorder without going through a microphone. Using a "patch" cord (or jumper) you come out of the

[1] The female portion of an electrical connection.

output jack in the source equipment and into the *line in* jack of your tape recorder. Then set the levels just as you did when you were using a microphone, and begin recording. The output jacks might be called *line out* they could also be called *monitor* or *external speaker*. Make sure you have a cord with the correct fittings on it, to mate with the jack you are connecting. There are several different types.

Cartridge Recorders

A piece of equipment that made the disk jockey's life considerably easier is the cartridge recorder, referred to in broadcasting as a *cart machine*. (See Figure 6-11.) It looks like a home eight-track tape player, but there are a few fundamental differences. A broadcast cart plays at a faster speed, and it does not have a built-in drive wheel. So tapes for the two are not interchangeable. For the most part, carts are used for short *spot announcements* rather than for music. They come loaded with varying lengths of tape, from 20 seconds to 30 minutes. Most commonly used are the 70-second carts, which are the right length for one-minute spot announcements. Their advantage over reel-to-reel tapes is that they can be taken out and put into the machine much more quickly. (See Figure 6-12.) The tape on a cart runs in a continuous loop. An automatic cuing device on the machine causes the tape to stop when it comes around to the beginning of the recorded announcement. Thus, the operator does not have to cue the tape manually, but simply slip it into the machine where it plays right from the beginning at the touch of a button. After the end of the spot, the tape continues to run until it arrives again at the

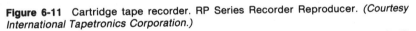

Figure 6-11 Cartridge tape recorder. RP Series Recorder Reproducer. *(Courtesy International Tapetronics Corporation.)*

Figure 6-12 Tape cartridge. *(Photo by Wayne Fogle.)*

beginning and stops automatically. Then it is ready for the next time it is used. A disadvantage of the cart machine is that it may have no fast-forward or rewind function. If it does not, you have to wait for it to recycle. It also has no erase head as does a reel-to-reel recorder. Before recording on a cart, therefore, it must be *bulk erased.*

Bulk Erasers

A bulk eraser is nothing more than an electromagnet. When it is turned on and a tape of any kind is placed in its electromagnetic field, all sound is erased from the tape. This procedure is always necessary before recording on a cart. It is advisable to do the same thing before recording on reel-to-reel tape. This will eliminate any unwanted, previously recorded sounds that might survive the erase head during the new recording. A word of caution: A bulk tape eraser can damage a watch that is not antimagnetic. Figure 6-13 shows a bulk tape eraser.

Audio Console

An audio console is the basic piece of equipment in master control (see Figure 6-14). All the other units are connected to it, so that you are able to mix and blend the sounds from each one. A console is sometimes called a *board* or a *mixer.* The outputs of turntables, tape recorders,

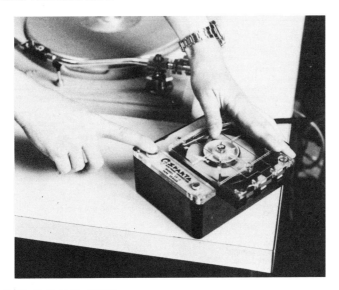

Figure 6-13 Bulk tape eraser.

microphones, and cart machines are connected to the console, with a channel switch and a volume control for each one. The volume control is called a *pot*. Normally master control is shaped in a horseshoe fashion. As the combo operator you would sit in the center with the console in front of you and the turntables on the sides. If the tape recorders are placed out of reach as they sometimes are, you would have remote control switches conveniently located for easy operation. The microphone would be on an adjustable boom, and you would set it at the appropriate distance. Now you are ready to work.

First, set the *level* on your microphone. You do this as described before by watching the VU meter on the front of the console. After you have cued your records and tapes, you are ready to go on the air.

Now, open your mike and begin talking. As you do, move your hands into position for your next operation. One hand should be on the switch that starts your turntable; the other hand should be on the *pot* that controls the volume. When you finish what you are saying, start the turntable and turn up the volume. Immediately check your VU meter to see that the music is at the same *level* as your voice. Then, turn off the mike. When you have learned to make these moves smoothly, you have become a disk jockey.

Note: The first time you do this you will be aware that when the mike is open you will not hear the music in the control room even though it is going out over the air. When the sound from a speaker goes back

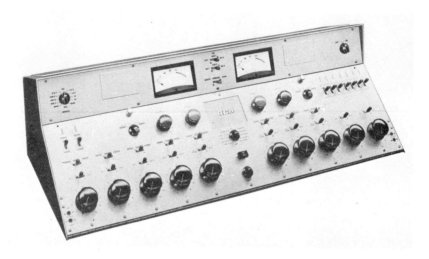

Figure 6-14 Audio Console. Model BC-7. *(Courtesy RCA.)*

into a microphone, a squealing noise results, that is called *feedback*. You may have heard this on public address systems. To prevent it, there is an automatic squelching device on the microphone switch to turn off the speaker in master control when the mike is on. So if you do not hear the music, be quiet until you have checked all your mike switches. You may be sorry if you utter an unairable expletive while you are trying to figure out what is wrong.

PATCH PANEL

There is one more part of master control operation you will have to learn, and that is *patching*. There are only a limited number of *pots* on your console; you may want to plug in something that is not part of the basic equipment. For example, you may want to put a phone call directly on the air. A *patch panel* (Figure 6-15) allows you to do this. It consists of several banks of holes, and cords that are called *patch cords*. One bank of holes will be *inputs;* another will be *outputs*. Let's say you want to put the telephone on pot No. 6 which is the one that controls your cart machine. You take a patch cord and come *out* of the hole labeled "telephone" and *in* to the one labeled "pot No. 6." Now pot No. 6 controls the volume of the telephone call on the air, rather than that of the cart machine. You do, of course, have to plan ahead, so that you do not tie up a piece of equipment that you will need later on.

These are the basic moves in combo operation. They may sound

Figure 6-15 Patch panel. *(Photo by Wayne Fogle.)*

easy to learn, and they are. However, there are many refinements that make the job one that requires considerable skill and timing. These you will acquire with experience and the direction of a competent engineer.

REMOTES

Your programming need not, in every case, originate from your own studios. It can come from anywhere the telephone company can install a line. A Class A broadcast line costs about the same as the installation of an ordinary telephone. You must, of course, order it well in advance and be specific about the location of the terminals. The equipment you need is a *remote amplifier and mixer.* Normally this unit comes with four microphone inputs. You could also attach a turntable to the remote unit. Picking up a remote simply involves connecting your equipment to the telephone line terminals, plugging in your microphones, and setting them in place. At the main studio you connect the telephone line to one of the output terminals of the patch panel, and patch into any of the channels on the main console. If you are the person at the remote site, you should have one of the microphones and a radio receiver, so you can listen for your *cue.* The cue should be prearranged and one that is clearly understood:

"Now here is Bill White at Buck Shaw Stadium in Santa Clara," says the studio announcer, turning up the pot that controls the remote, and you, at the other end, begin talking. With remote units you can pick up sporting events, concerts, lectures, discussions, city council meetings, and a variety of other activities. The fact that the program is live and direct gives it much more appeal than it would have if it were recorded.

RECORDED PROGRAMS

Not all of the programs you hear on the radio are *live*. In the old days (prior to World War II) the FCC had strict rules about announcing that a program was *transcribed*.[2] Since then the regulations have been relaxed, because the public has come to expect that much of what they hear will be on tape. Before the age of tape recorders, the programs were produced on large disks called *electrical transcriptions*. Occasionally we still use the expression *ET* to mean a program or spot announcement on a record. Tape and carts, however, are much more practical. They are cheaper and can be used over and over.

There are several reasons why you would want to produce a program on tape rather than do it live. One is that you can play it again on other occasions. Also, you can stop in the middle if you make a mistake and do a portion of it over. Usually the recorded program uses materials from a variety of sources; doing it live would mean assembling all the people in one place at one time. The program you produce may involve interviews with several different people who have never been in the same room together. You can have all of these on separate tapes and then select the statements from each you think are most relevant. One way to do this would be to dub each statement on to a long cart just as described in making spot announcements. Then you can sit down at the console with records on the turntables, your microphone, and the recorded interviews on the cart machine. You would probably want to have a script or an outline in front of you rather than try to ad lib. From this point on the steps would be something like this:

1 Bulk-erase a reel-to-reel tape, and "thread it up" on the recorder.
2 Start recording, and let the tape run about 30 seconds before you put any sound on it.
3 Start the music at full volume, fade it down, open your mike and read your introduction. Bring the music up briefly; then fade it under and out.

[2] Another term for "recorded."

4 Begin your own speech and when you come to a point where you want one of the previously recorded statements, push the start button on the cart machine. Make sure the channel switch is on and the volume is turned up.

5 Continue through the program in this fashion, always watching your VU meter. Be sure that your levels are constant; you want your music and pretaped interviews at the same volume as your voice.

6 At the end of the program close all the channels and let the reel-to-reel tape continue to record for a full minute. This will assure that any previously recorded material on the tape will be erased. Can you see the problem? If you stopped the tape immediately at the end, and there were other sounds on the tape, what would happen when the tape was played back on the air?

A few words of caution: Make sure to wind back and erase any false starts on the tape. For example, you may start once, make a mistake, and start again. If you leave the first start on the tape, the operator may cue it up to that point when it is put on the air. Remember to label your tape, giving the speed, the length, the date, and your name as producer.

PRODUCTION SPOTS

Sometimes spot announcements will be recorded in a production studio. A sponsor may want a message that is "produced," perhaps with music, sound effects, and several voices. The recorded spot also assures that the announcement will not be misread on the air. The copy itself might be written by the salesperson or by some other member of the staff. It could also have been prepared by an advertising agency or the parent company of a participating sponsor. The copy would then go to the production or operations director, who might give it to you, as a staff announcer, to record. You might want to read it "straight" without anything added to the copy, or you might wish to dress it up a bit. You could do any of the following:

Use two or more voices to add variety
Read it through an echo chamber
Add recorded music or sound effects
Dramatize it

These embellishments are possible only if the spot is recorded. It may take several tries before you get it the way you want it. It is not unusual to spend several hours producing one 60-second spot. If the account is going to run frequently and for a long time, you will want to make several different ones for variety. You may want to put them all on the same cart or each on a separate one. Having them on separate carts gives the traffic director the ability to select certain ones for certain times of the day.

When doing production work there are a few things to remember: Most cart machines do not have an erase head; many do not have fast forward or reverse. This can be an inconvenience. If you are putting three spots on one cart you may get the first two perfectly, and make a mistake on the third. Then you would have to bulk-erase the whole cart and start over. For this reason it is a better plan to record all three spots on reel-to-reel tape first; then *dub*[3] them off onto a cart. When you dub, *cue* the reel-to-reel tape to the start of the announcement. Then put a *bulk-erased* cart in the cartridge recorder and put it in record mode. On the console open the channel and turn up the pot that controls the reel-to-reel tape. This will connect the *output* of the reel-to-reel machine to the *input* of the cart machine. Then start both machines at the same time. The spot will be recorded on the cart from the very start. When the spot ends, stop the reel-to-reel tape and let the cart machine run until it recycles back to the start of the spot. It will automatically stop at the beginning. You can record as many spots as the cart will contain. When the machine is in record mode, each time you push the start button a cue is placed on the tape. On playback it will always stop at each of those cues.

Here is an example of the copy written for a production spot:

MUSIC:	"ENTRANCE OF THE GLADIATOR"—UP THREE SECONDS AND FADE
BARKER:	Hurry, Hurry! Step right up folks, the big show is about to begin. All the action is on the inside. . .
ANNOUNCER:	Wait a minute. When it comes to the circus all the action may be on the inside, but the impression you make happens on the outside. Clothes may not "make the man," but they are mighty important and Westgate Men's Wear is going to help you do something about that fall wardrobe of yours. Right now men's corduroy sport coats are on sale at $39.95—contrasting slacks starting at just $14.95. There are sport shirts in a variety of styles and colors that are marked down 30 to 50 per cent. The sale will last this week only, so. . .
BARKER:	Hurry, Hurry, Hurry! Right this way for the big show. The wild animals will amaze you. . .
ANNOUNCER:	. . .And so will the sale items at Westgate Men's Wear—located in the Westgate Shopping Center in Midtown. You'll save a tentful of money, and I'm not lyin'.
SOUND:	LION ROAR

[3] Transfer material from one recording device to another.

Much of your work at a radio station will involve production. You may spend as many hours in the production studio as you do in master control. In addition to producing commercial and public service announcements, you may also want to make promotion spots for the station. This is generally referred to as *station continuity* and consists of material on tape that can be played periodically during the day to promote particular programs. There is a lot you can do in a production studio. Sometimes it is frustrating when you are unable to get just exactly the effect you want, but it is challenging and always stimulating.

SUMMARY

The equipment you will use in master control at a broadcasting studio is similar to that which you may already have used if you are a hi-fi buff. One difference is that your home units are probably high impedance while professional broadcasting equipment is low impedance. With practice you will be able to operate the equipment with facility so that you can give full attention to what you are saying on the air. The tools of your trade are the console and patch panel, microphones, turntables, and reel-to-reel and cartridge tape recorders. You will be using both kinds of tape machine in your on-the-air work and in your recorded productions.

TERMINOLOGY

Audio console
Back timing
Bidirectional microphone
Bulk eraser
Cardioid microphone
Cartridge tape recorder
  (cart machine)
Cart (tape)
Condenser microphone
Cue
Cuing amplifier
Cross fade
Dead air
Dynamic (pressure) microphone
ET (electrical transcription)
False starts
Feedback
Gain
High impedance

Input jack
Ips (inches per second)
Lavalier microphone
Level
Load
Low impedance
Master control
Mixer
Monitor (speaker)
Music under
Omnidirectional microphone
Output jack
Patch panel
Ribbon (velocity) microphone
Segue
Unidirectional microphone
VU (volume unit) meter
Windscreen
Zero level

ACTIVITIES

1 Using your home equipment, dub the music from a record onto a reel-to-reel tape. If you have a hi-fi set there are probably jacks in the back labeled "output," "monitor," or "speaker." Possibly there is an earphone jack. Any of these can be used as an output. Attach a cord from one of these to the input of your tape recorder. The input might be labeled "line in" or "aux in." See if there is much loss in fidelity when you dub from the record to the tape.

2 Produce a program of poetry readings. Start by recording several short selections on one reel-to-reel tape. Use different voices if possible; allow a few seconds pause after each selection. Now write an introduction, giving the program a title and a theme. Select instrumental music you think would be appropriate to play under each poem. If you have access to a production studio with an audio console, follow the steps on pages 72 to 73 blending your own voice with the music and the other voices on tape.

3 Record a series of short sound effects on cart. You can produce them "live"— with a microphone—by slamming doors and ringing bells, or you can dub them from other recordings. Sit down at the console with your microphone open. Push the button on the cart machine for each sound and see if you can ad lib a reaction to each one. Record the whole procedure on a reel-to-reel tape. Do the same exercise with another set of sound effects that someone else records for you. Keep your cues tight and your responses fast and short.

Keeping the Logs

OPERATING AND PROGRAM LOGS

The operator of a broadcasting station is required to keep two logs: the *operating log* and the *program log*. In the operating log you must show the time the carrier (transmitter) was turned on and the time modulation (program) began. Each broadcast day must begin with a *sign-on*. This is an announcement which includes the call letters of the station and the name of the city where the station is licensed. Generally the sign-on also states the operating frequency, channel number, and radiated power of the station as well as the names of the owners. When the station signs off, the same information is given. The operating log also includes meter readings, which must be taken every three hours. Required meter readings vary from one station to another; the procedure will be explained to you by the chief engineer.

The program log serves two functions: (1) It provides a guide for the operator so he or she will know what programs and spot announcements

PROGRAM LOG

SCHEDULED TIME	PROGRAMS–ANNOUNCEMENTS	TIME		PROGRAMS		ANNOUNCEMENTS		INITIALS
		ON	OFF	SOURCE	TYPE	LENGTH	TYPE	$J.H.$
8:00	I-D	8^{00}						
8:00	The Rock Allen Show	8^{00}	8^{30}	REC	E			
	Kelly's Hardware(cart B-8)	8^{06}				:30	COM	
	Red Rose Florist(live)	8^{14}				1:00	COM	
	Full Employment Council(live)	8^{21}				:30	PSA	
	Election Coverage(cart R-3)	8^{22}				:45	SC	
8:30	I-D	8^{30}						
8:30	News	8^{30}	8^{35}	L	N			
8:35	Sports Round-up	8^{35}	8^{45}	L	S			
8:45	Local Government Report	8^{45}	9^{00}	L	PA			
9:00	I-D	9^{00}						
9:00	Music til Midnight	9^{00}	9^{30}	REC	E			
	Goodwill Industries(live)	9^{08}				:30	PSA	
	Freeman's Malt Shop(live)	9^{18}				1:00	COM	
	Passtime Motel(cart G-2)	9^{21}				:30	COM	
9:30	I-D	9^{30}						
9:30	News Headlines	9^{30}	9^{33}	L	N			
9:32	Music til Midnight	9^{33}	10^{00}	REC	E			
	Mental Health Assoc(live)	9^{41}				:30	PSA	
	Salvation Army(cart H-3)	9^{52}				:45	PSA	
								$J.H.$

REMARKS:

Figure 7-1 Program log.

have been scheduled for the day, and (2) it serves as a record that can be made available to a sponsor, the FCC, or the general public. The FCC requires that logs be kept accurately and legibly. If a sponsor wants to know when a commercial announcement was run, you should be able to find it in the log. And don't log it if you didn't run it! If you do, you can be charged with fraud. Remember, *your* name is in the log, and you, personally, can be held responsible, as well as the station. Program logs become part of the *public file.* Anyone may come into the station and ask to see them. They should be kept neatly and maintained in an organized fashion. An FCC inspector may come in to see the logs, too. If there is reason to suspect improper conduct, the inspector may tape a portion of the broadcast day, and then check to see if it coincides with the log for that period. If falsifications are found, both the station and the operator can be issued a citation and asked to explain the discrepancy. If the explanation is not satisfactory, and if the transgression is serious, both station and operator may lose their licenses. I have known cases where operators have been fired for not keeping logs properly. In one case, the logs had been filled out in advance. The young man was discovered, much to his chagrin, when the station suffered a power outage and went off the air after the logs had already been filled out. It would be a shame to have your career interrupted like this over a technicality, especially when keeping logs is such a simple task.

The style of program logs will vary, but the essential elements will be constant. (See Figure 7-1). In the center of the log will be a space for *programs* and *announcements*. Every item entered must be one or the other; none may be both. Each must be accompanied by specific information.

PROGRAMS: TYPE AND SOURCE

Almost anything can be classified as a program, but usually it is something that is 2 minutes or more in length. In the log will be a space for the *type* of program and its *source*.

Type

The log must tell how the program is classified, or its type. The following are the ones generally recognized:

E   Light *entertainment:* such as popular music.

N   *News:* current events presented without emphasis on any particular point of view.

PA   *Public affairs:* discussion programs, talk shows, etc.

GEN   *General education:* cultural programs offered for the general enlightenment of the listener.

I   *Instructional:* programs offered by educational institutions for academic credit.

EDIT   *Editorial:* programs expressing the point of view of the station.

POL   *Political:* programs that endorse political candidates.

S   *Sports:* reporting or actual play by play.

R   *Religious:* church services or church news

AG   *Agriculture:* news about farms, crops, etc.

A radio station should be conscientious about providing the appropriate classification for each program. Every three years the license must be renewed, and the FCC will ask for a breakdown in percent of the amount of time devoted to the various program types. If everything is *light entertainment,* there may be a question about the station's responsibility in providing a public service. The station owner must remember that licenses can be challenged every time they come up for renewal.

Source

The log must tell where the program originates. The following symbols are the ones most commonly used:

L   *Local* means that the program was produced at the station, utilizing live talent more than 50 percent of the time.

NET   *Network* means that the program is originating from a distant location and being fed to the local station. In this case the designation might also be the initials of a network: NBC, CBS, ABC, etc.

REC   *Recorded* means that 50 percent or more of the program material has been previously recorded. Most disk jockey programs would have this designation.

REM   *Remote* refers to a program originating from a location away from the main studios. The program material is produced by station personnel, but it is not coming from the place where the station is licensed. A remote might come from a local sports arena or shopping center. The sound is received at the station by telephone line or shortwave transmission and then broadcast in the normal fashion.

ANNOUNCEMENTS: TYPE AND DURATION

An entry on the log that is called an announcement (or spot) is usually a minute or less in length. It should have a designation indicating its *type* and its *duration.*

Type

The following are symbols commonly used:

COM   *Commercial* indicates a spot announcement that has been paid for by a sponsor.

PSA   *Public service announcement* is a message for which no charge has been made and which presents information about a non-profit organization or cause that is in the public interest.

SC   *Station continuity* is an announcement that provides information about the radio station itself, such as promotion for a special program.

Duration

The length of a spot announcement may be important. For example, on a commercial station a 30-second announcement will cost less than one that runs a full minute. In the column in the log that calls for duration, the length of the spot should be entered in minutes and seconds. Use a colon to separate the two as follows:

1:00—to indicate 1 minute
:30—to indicate 30 seconds

The job of preparing the program log is done by the *traffic director,* who will type into the log all the programs and spot announcements, with their *scheduled times,* prior to the broadcast day. As the operator, you will receive the log with most of the information already entered. Your job will be to write in the *actual time* that the programs and spots are run. Programs need both *time on* and *time off;* spot announcements need only *time on* because their duration has already been indicated.

TRAFFIC DIRECTOR

If there is one person on a radio station staff who is in a position to see the entire picture, it is the traffic director. Primarily the job involves preparing the daily program log, and so the traffic director has to be familiar with all the programs and spot announcements and must know something about the skills of all the other members of the staff. The traffic director works with the program director in laying out the format for each broadcast day. He or she must be informed when programs are changed and is often consulted about time availabilities, program content, and listener response. The traffic director works very closely with the sales personnel, who supply information about what air time the sponsor wants and how many commercials to insert. It is the responsibility of the traffic director to offer *protection* for sponsors whenever possible. This means keeping competitive spots separated. In addition, there is a broadcasters' code that calls for not putting more than 18 minutes of commercials into any one hour. The traffic director should have a thorough understanding of the *rate card,* which is a directive that tells the cost of the station's spot announcements. Some times of the day are more expensive than others; if a sponsor is paying for *prime time,* that sponsor's spot must be run at prime time. Although it may never be necessary for the traffic director to talk on the radio or hold a license, he or she should know something about combo operation and have an understanding of what the combo person can and cannot do. Programs or spot announcements must not be put in an impossible sequence. The traffic director also works with management, and needs to be informed about bookkeeping and billing.

In recent years, the burden of the traffic director has been eased considerably by the use of computers. A computer program can be designed so that the printout contains the information needed by the accounting department for billing purposes as well as the programming department for scheduling and keeping records.

Preparing the program log is only half the responsibility of the traffic director. The other half is to see that all the copy, tapes, and transcriptions that are written into the log are actually in the control room where they are supposed to be. If the operator has to cross out a commercial because the copy or tape was not available, the station loses revenue. The traffic director must see that it is in place and that it is *current*. Often sponsors like to change their copy regularly. There is no point in reading a commercial about a sale that has already passed. When new copy is prepared, the old copy has to come out, or else the announcer may read it by mistake. It is especially important for the traffic director to keep the carts up to date, because you don't know what they say until you play them.

Labeling Carts

On the front edge of every cart, the traffic director will place a sticker. It will give the name of the sponsor (or public service organization) the way it appears on the log. There will also be a number or a letter to identify it and facilitate filing. That will be on the log and on the label. If there is a termination time for the spot, the label may contain a "kill" date. And if there is any room left, the label will have the last few words of the announcement. This is called the "out cue." A label on a cart may look something like this:

> B-8 *Kelly's Hardware* Kill: Jan 16
> Cue: ". . . this Jan. sales event."

In the program log the traffic director would write *Kelly's Hardware-Cart B-8.* All of this information is necessary. The name of the sponsor has to appear because just a letter and a number would not be understandable to the FCC or the general public if they looked at the log a year later. The log must also contain the information necessary for the operator to know how to find the spot and whether it is live or recorded. The out cue on the cart tells the announcer when it is time to come in with the next record or live comment. The procedure and filing system may vary from one station to another, but the practice is basically the same.

Live Copy

There are several different ways of working with live copy. Usually each of the commercials that the announcer will have to read is placed in a loose-leaf binder. This way it can be moved and changed easily. The copy would be alphabetized and sometimes given a code letter similar to that which appeared on the cart. This might be necessary if there is more than one piece of copy that the sponsor is running. *Kelly's Hardware* would be filed under K for Kelly rather than H for Hardware. There must be a convention that is understood by both the operator and the traffic director.

Live Tags

Often commercials or public service announcements are prepared by large advertising agencies in a distant city. There may be hundreds of different outlets and merchants that handle the product. So the advertising agency must rely on the local station to provide the specific information about where the item is available. Kelly's Hardware, for example, may carry General Electric products. GE will send Kelly advertising materials that he can use as he wishes—posters, display stands, etc. They may also send him a vinyl disk (formerly called an electrical transcription, or ET for short) with several different spots on separate cuts. They may vary in length and content. The parent company may pay part or all of the cost if Kelly wishes to advertise on the local radio station. If so, the station would play the designated cut on the ET and then add a "live tag" that tells the listener that the product is available at Kelly's Hardware. The live tag is treated the same as any other piece of copy. But the traffic director must be sure to include the information in the log that there is a tag that goes with the ET. The combo operator must be ready for this too. It is easy to forget about the tag. I am sure you have heard announcers who have.

SUMMARY

Keeping logs is an important part of your job as a combo operator. The chief engineer at the station where you work will show you how to make entries in the operator's log. Program logs will vary from one station to another, but you should have an understanding of the basic principles. Keep in mind that the program log has two functions: to serve as a *guide* for the operator, and to provide a *record* of what programs and spot announcements the station aired. Knowing how to prepare program logs will help you get a job as a traffic director—a position that may not be glamourous, but is extremely important. The traffic director's job is not finished when the entry is made in the log; he or she must see that all tapes and copy are properly labeled and in the control room where they are supposed to be. The traffic director's job is one of the main determinants of a station's smooth operation.

TERMINOLOGY

Copy	Prime time
Format	Protection
Kill date	PSA
Live	Spot
Out cue	Tag

ACTIVITIES

1 Prepare a blank program log that looks like the one shown on page 78. Select a station in your community and listen to it for a period of two hours. As you listen, log all the programs and announcements that you hear. Be as accurate as you can in writing down the times. Call the station and ask if you can compare your log with theirs. They should be willing to accommodate you, as the logs are part of their public file. It might be a good idea, however, to tell them you are doing this as a class exercise. Be sure you note how the station has classified each of the programs and spot announcements.

2 Ask to see the station's latest license renewal application. (This is also part of the public file.) See what percentage of the station's total air time was devoted to each of the various program types.

3 Talk to the traffic director. Find out what system the station uses for labeling carts, logging spots, and making copy available to announcers. Ask what their method is for keeping track of where the spots go and how long they are to run. If possible, visit the control room to see how the copy is filed and where the tapes and carts are kept.

Programming the Station

RADIO PROGRAMMING FORMATS

Every radio station must have a programming structure which is called the *format*. The format may also be called the *sound*, and stations generally prefer to maintain a certain degree of consistency so that listeners will know what to expect. Highly structured stations will have a very rigid format, meaning that disk jockeys and announcers have little flexibility regarding what they say and what music they play. A loose format is one that allows the air personalities to exercise some creative expression in terms of their music and ad lib remarks. Programming is the most important aspect of radio station operation. The message that is communicated is, after all, the central reason for all of the technological talents and energies that go into sound transmission. In radio your choice is limited to the auditory stimulus. Your message can be in the form of speech or music. The task is simplified considerably for the station that selects music as its basic format, because there is so much available in recorded form. A station that selects a talk format must plan on maintaining a much larger staff and spending considerably more money for writers and announcers. Every station must have some talk, and most utilize some recorded music. The decisions regarding the amount of talk and the kind of music are made by the programming department.

THE PROGRAM DIRECTOR

The programming department is headed by the program director. He or she works closely with the manager, and perhaps the owners of the station, to effect a policy that would result in a fluid and balanced sound. As noted in the organization chart in Chapter 1, the program director supervises the announcers and combo operators and usually has influence over the newscasters, although some station managers prefer to give the news department a high degree of autonomy. Being charged with maintaining the quality of the station's sound, the program director usually has the power to hire and fire personnel.

If you are preparing yourself for the job of program director, you should start right away. You need a broad background and extensive experience in all phases of broadcasting. You should be able to understand, if not perform, all the jobs of the other staff members. You may not need a first class license, but you will need to understand what the engineer tells you about the equipment. You might need to help make decisions as to what equipment the station should purchase. And remember that the quality and performance of the equipment is going to have a significant effect on the sound of the station. You will have to know the capabilities of the equipment in order to develop effectively the sound that you want. You certainly would find it necessary to have had the experience of a combo operator so that you could direct and perform operations of the production studio and master control. If you were program director of a large station, your job would perhaps be mostly administrative and supervisory. But at smaller stations it is likely that you would be on the air and also do some production work. You would have to know something about the business aspects of the station, and you might be consulted in managerial decisions. As program director you would also be working closely with the sales manager. You would need to know about the marketability of the product for which you are responsible. You would need to understand ratings and how to interpret audience surveys. It may be that your job would depend upon your ability to make a respectable showing when the surveys are conducted. You have to listen to other stations besides your own so that you are aware of trends and apprised of what the competition is doing. Even more than the announcers and combo operators, you must understand current tastes—not only in music, but in topics of interest. You are the one who would be responsible for establishing the tone of the station and consequently the type of audience that will be attracted to it.

In addition to getting people to listen to the station, you must also perform the logistical functions necessary to the station. It will be your job to schedule the announcers and combo operators and to deploy the personnel in the most efficient manner. For example, one disk jockey may be more effective in the morning than at night, and you will want to utilize her or his talents to the fullest. You may also want to avoid voice "blends" and try to separate voices that sound too much alike. Other logistical responsibilities include the scheduling of programs and spot announcements. You would have to feed information to the traffic director who would prepare the log each day and make any necessary changes or additions.

As program director you would also have to be well informed on the FCC's *Rules and Regulations.* You would have to understand the responsibilities of the broadcaster as described in Chapter 2. If you were scheduling a political debate you would have to be aware of the conditions contained in section 315 of the Communications Act. You would have to recognize that the FCC can and does levy fines against broadcasting stations for improper programming practices. Infractions such as obscenity and conducting lotteries on the air are, you will recall, violations of the penal code as well as FCC regulations. So the areas of responsibility assigned to the program director are extensive.

As program director you would decide not only the style of music and the format, but you would also select the personnel to effect it. You may choose to hire experienced air personalities and allow them to use their own judgment when they are working. One station that operates this way is KSFO in San Francisco. The disk jockeys pick their own music and present it in their own way, each with an individual style. The station is quite successful financially. It is promoted as an adult station and one that listeners can tune to all day without hearing the same musical selections repeated. This method works well, but requires highly paid personalities. If you are operating on a limited budget, you may not be able to afford it. You may also wish to maintain some control over the sound of the station so that there is consistency. One device that is commonly used is the "hot" clock (see Figure 8-1). This provides the disk jockey with a guide on what to play and what to say.

Sometimes programming is a function of necessity. The music is selected from the records available to the station; the style of presentation is determined by the talents and interests of the personnel. On other

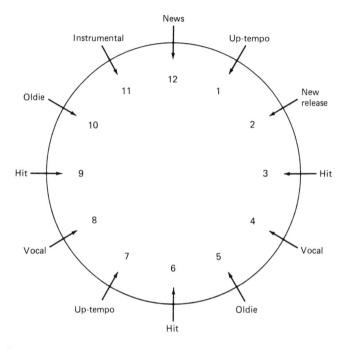

Figure 8-1 Hot clock indicates what type of record to play in each 5-minute segment.

occasions you may be tempted to program to your own tastes and play the kind of music you personally like to hear. These methods are questionable and will succeed only if you are very lucky. There are two qualities you must have as program director: some knowledge in a variety of fields and a sense of what other people find interesting and entertaining. Only then will you be able to make choices. Subject matter and musical styles that are outside your frame of reference are not available to you as programming possibilities. The broader your base the greater selection you have. One word of caution, however: Remember that just because something is different does not mean it is good. You can put any kind of weird or abhorrent sound on the air and you will be able to find someone who likes it. You must rely upon your own judgment as well as the response you get from the audience.

NETWORK PROGRAMMING

Networks play a much less significant role in radio programming today than they used to. At one time radio stations relied very heavily upon the networks for program content, and the most popular stations were those that had network affiliations. This condition no longer prevails. Relatively few stations are affiliated with networks, and often the most popular stations are independent. Network offerings are almost entirely news and public affairs, and these are not the greatest attractions to large numbers of listeners.

Most people are familiar with the three major networks, ABC, CBS, and NBC. But there are smaller ones, such as the Mutual Broadcasting System, which also provide services to radio stations. It is important to know that a station may be affiliated with a network without being owned by it. No individual or corporation may own more than seven of any kind of broadcasting station. When we say that a radio station is an *affiliate* of NBC we mean that they are under an agreement to provide services for each other. NBC may actually *own* as many as seven AM and seven FM radio stations but may be feeding programs to several hundred affiliates. The network will give an exclusive franchise to just one station in a given area. There would not be two or more NBC stations competing against each other, for example. When a station becomes affiliated with a network, it agrees to make a certain amount of its air time available for the broadcasting of network programs. The time is sold to the network at a reduced rate. In other words, the station receives revenue for the air time, but not as much as it would receive from its own advertisers. The advantage to the station is that it obtains the prestige of having nationally prominent personalities present the news or other program material. Network newscasts generally have more credibility than those produced by local newscasters.

The Network Affiliate

A station that becomes a network affiliate agrees to carry certain programs as a package, including the commercial announcements. This agreement is necessary because the network is obtaining its revenue from sponsors who purchase time with the understanding that their messages will be aired at certain times by a certain number of stations. The more affiliates a network has, the more extensive will be its coverage, and the more it will be able to charge for spot announcements. National network coverage is very expensive and is proportional to the size of the audience. Some network programs are provided on an optional basis. The affiliate may carry them or not, as it chooses. In some cases, the network may allow the affiliate to "cut away" from the program long enough to insert its own commercial spot announcements.

The term *network* does not necessarily imply coast-to-coast coverage, although we usually think of it that way. A network may consist of just a few stations in a given region, all broadcasting the same program. Certain sporting events, for example, might be very popular in certain regions but would not warrant coast-to-coast coverage. At one time baseball received national coverage, but now even major league games are of interest only to fans in the immediate vicinity. Network programs originate from a particular location and are fed to affiliated stations by means of telephone lines. The network does not do the transmitting; that is done by each local station in its own area.

For the combo operator, network programming requires considerable skill and excellent timing. Network programs are fed to all affiliated stations simultaneously. The traffic director will schedule the times for each program, and this information will appear in the log. The operator must be able to plan ahead so that the local program will end in time for the start of the network program. A network newscast, for example, will begin precisely on the hour and the operator must be ready to throw the switch to bring it in within one or two seconds of the scheduled time. On some occasions the program may be tape-recorded for release at a later time, but more often the network program is broadcast live.

THE INDEPENDENT STATION

An independent station is one that is not affiliated with a network. It may utilize tapes or transcriptions produced by outside agencies, but for the most part its programming is generated through its own efforts. Most independent stations rely heavily upon recorded music; all-news stations need the support and resources of network facilities. Programming an independent station is challenging and creative. Among the vast number of possible choices available, those you make will depend on several factors.

Size of the Market

The number of people in your listening range is important, because it will determine how likely it is that you will be able to get an audience for the program offerings you select. In a large metropolitan area you would probably be able to draw a sufficient audience for almost any kind of programming you might choose. Foreign language programs, for example, would be possible in New York or Chicago, but perhaps not in a small Midwestern town.

Competition

If you are going into a multistation market, you will have to consider what kind of programming is being offered by the competition. If other

stations are doing an effective job of reaching the major audience segments, you may choose to offer an alternative—for the minority whose
tastes are different. Instead of playing the current popular hits, you
could offer concert music or ethnic programs.

Regional Tastes

Some parts of the country have strong preferences for certain kinds of
music. Recognize, of course, that these tastes are subject to change and
that there are dangers in overgeneralizing. Country and western music is
probably more popular in the Southwestern states than on the East or
West Coast. There are other types of music that may be associated with
certain areas: Rocky Mountain music, hillbilly music, and sacred hymns
are examples of music that are perhaps more acceptable in some regions
than in others.

Resources of the Station

Your programming may be limited by your own resources. The low-
budget station is not going to be able to do the elaborate programming
that is possible for a large station with a well-paid staff. Personality disk
jockeys who are themselves entertainers are able to command big salaries which you may not be able to pay. The same is true for writers and
newscasters. Unless you have a large staff of highly professional people,
you will probably choose to program more music and less talk.

Mode of Transmission

One of the most significant determinants of programming is the mode of
transmission. FM and AM have different characteristics and these differences are often reflected in the programming of the station. Because
of the dimension of stereo, FM lends itself to music better than AM. FM
stations usually try to capitalize on this advantage by offering more music and less talk. Let us take a more detailed look at the differences
between these two types of transmission.

AM AND FM TRANSMISSION

AM and FM are two different modes of transmission. FM produces
clearer sounds than AM, but the waves do not travel as far. FM waves
travel in straight lines and do not go over obstacles as well as AM waves.
Consequently an FM station, even one of extremely high power, will not
cover as wide an area as an AM station of comparable power. If you
have an FM set in your car, you may have noticed considerably more
fading of the signal with it than occurs in AM. In fact there are times

when one station may suddenly disappear altogether and another one take its place on the dial.

While more and more cars are being equipped with FM receivers, their performance is marginal in many areas, where mountains or atmospheric conditions impede reception. Also, FM receivers are adversely affected by automobile ignition systems; there often is considerable interference in the midst of heavy or congested traffic. These limitations in the reception of FM have a significant effect upon the financial condition, and consequently the programming, of a station. During commuting hours (sometimes called *drive times*) AM has a definite advantage over FM. Furthermore, these hours have become the most critical ones for sustaining a listening audience. When television became the dominant medium during the evening hours, radio had to find an audience at a different time of the day. The answer came in the form of car and portable radios. It is possible to carry the sound medium with you wherever you go, but so far television has not enjoyed this degree of portability. Commuting time became a heavy radio-listening period. Most AM stations regard the hours of 6 to 9 A.M. and 4 to 6 P.M. as their "prime time" and charge more for their spot announcements during these periods. FM listening is still heaviest in the home during the late morning and afternoon hours. There is often a significant rise after 3 P.M., when school lets out.

With the exception of drive time, FM probably has more listeners than AM. But remember that the FM band is much wider. In any given locale, there are perhaps twice as many FM stations as AM. In a large metropolitan area a listening audience may be divided among fifteen AM stations but as many as thirty or forty FM stations. Generally an AM station, because of drive time and broader area of coverage, will have more listeners than an FM station. In order to compete, the FM station must not only charge less for each spot announcement, but must carry fewer commercials in order to retain its audience. In prime time an AM station may run from fifteen to eighteen commercial announcements per hour. Most FM stations choose not to have more than six or eight spots in the same time period. Often the FM station will run announcements in clusters (double or triple spotting) in order to allow for a continuous flow of uninterrupted music.

Programming is also affected by the physical characteristics of the two media. During commuting hours the bulk of the AM listeners are in cars on their way to work, so those stations are inclined to offer news and weather and traffic reports. While some FM stations may also do this, they recognize their limitations and tend to rely on what they can do best: offer stereo music. Some people in broadcasting believe that AM radio will someday consist entirely of talk and FM entirely of music. An extreme position, but the point of view emphasizes the strengths of each of the media. The sound quality of music transmitted in FM stereo is outstanding, and it is not likely that AM will ever be able to compete with it.

THE TARGET AUDIENCE

The target audience consists of the people you would like to acquire as listeners. You want them not only to listen, but also to buy the products of your sponsors. So the size of the audience is important, but their purchasing power is even more important. Generally speaking, the largest audience segment is the teenage audience, but their purchasing power is not as great as that of older people. You can reach the teenage audience (sometimes referred to as the "bubble gum set") by playing the current popular hits. This kind of station is often called a "top 40" station, in reference to their choice of musical fare. Top 40 stations usually have the highest ratings in terms of numbers of listeners, but they are not necessarily the most profitable. A station that is able to draw an older, more mature audience may be more effective in advertising higher-priced, quality merchandise, and consequently be able to charge more for spot announcements. There are advantages, however, in having high ratings. Advertisers are impressed by numbers of listeners regardless of the age bracket, and the station may be able to sell more spots—at least for products that appeal to teenagers.

Radio broadcasting is a highly competitive business. In a large metropolitan area you could be up against forty or fifty other stations. All of them are trying to attract and hold a particular audience segment, and all of them will be attempting to do it in their own unique way. Some stations may have a few loyal fans who listen to one station exclusively, but more frequently listeners will switch from one station to another. There may be five or six stations that the average listener will tune to on a regular basis—about the same number as there are push buttons on a car radio. Most stations will select a particular type of music to form their basic sound. They may mix and blend a number of different types, but they will usually attempt to maintain a certain degree of consistency.

TYPES OF MUSIC STATIONS

The classification of musical types may be an injustice to the arts, but radio broadcasters find it useful to establish terminology to describe what they are doing. The terms listed here are the ones commonly used in the industry and are by no means inclusive of all musical types. Some musical selections defy classification, and others may fall into more than one category.

Top 40   This is the term commonly used to refer to the current, popular hits. The style of music will change depending upon what happens to be in vogue. It consists of the selections that are most popular in terms of requests and record sales. Top 40 stations are perhaps the most common because they appeal to the largest audience segment.

Easy Listening   This is light concert and popular music that is melodious and harmonious. The music is mostly instrumental rather than vocal. It is the type that is often called "background" or "mood" music and is frequently heard in supermarkets and office buildings.

MOR   This stands for "middle of the road." It is similar to "easy listening" but contains some hits and more vocals. Usually it is up-tempo with a mild rock beat and some discotheque rhythms.

Progressive   This is current music and is relatively avant-garde and experimental. It is the type of music that is often played at rock concerts. Progressive music is sometimes called "AOR," standing for album-oriented rock. It is designed to be played very loud and often utilizes special sound effects created by electronic instruments.

Country-Western   Sometimes this type of music is referred to by its initials, C-W. It is music in the tradition of *The Grand Ole Opry*. There is a heavy emphasis on the steel guitar and vocals in a southwestern accent. Hillbilly music might be regarded as a subheading under country and western.

Folk   This is a broad category that can include contemporary music as well as traditional. It is music of the people, often ballads and story-telling songs. The emphasis in folk music is generally upon the words and the message conveyed in the lyrics.

Classical   The term "classical music" usually refers to serious music that has survived for several generations. It is the type of music that is played by symphony orchestras in concert halls. It also includes chamber music and opera.

Jazz   This is a type of music that defies description. We think of it as that which comes from the American tradition, and more specifically, the southern black culture. It is highly rhythmical and often free-form music. It is frequently improvised and performed at a feeling level.

Ethnic   With the recent increase in specialization, there has been an influx of stations that appeal to various ethnic groups. This category includes the music of foreign countries. Spanish programming is perhaps the most prevalent, but there are also stations that specialize in German, French, Greek, and other styles of music from distant places.

Religious   Churches and religious organizations often provide considerable financial support to radio stations. Religious or sacred music is programming fare that can be heard in many locations throughout the country. There is enough variety in Christian music so that stations of this type do not have to be overly repetitious.

This list is intended as an index of terminology rather than as a denotation of musical types. The specific selections included under each of these headings will vary considerably from one program director to another.

THE MUSIC DIRECTOR

Radio stations have a symbiotic relationship with record distributors; each contributes to and depends upon the other. Radio stations must have records. This is their stock in trade. They could not afford to buy all the records they need because music changes so rapidly. The distributors' business is to sell records to the general public, and to do this they must get "air play." Therefore, they are happy to provide radio stations with sample copies as long as the station agrees to play them. One radio station staff member will serve as music director. This person has the job of keeping in touch with record distributors by letter, phone, and personal contact. He or she will provide information the distributor needs: what records are being played, which are requested most, how often a selection is repeated, etc. The best service is provided to the stations that are conscientious about making this information available. Sometimes stations mail out weekly *play lists.* These are complete accounts of the music that was aired during the week. Distributors then know what type of records to send to the stations. Sometimes distributors will encourage stations by allowing them to be the first to release a potentially "hot" record. On the other hand a station may exercise its own leverage by boycotting a company that does not provide good record service. So the relationship depends upon cooperation. It is important for the distributor to know what kind of records the station plays. Some stations, for example, play only albums, not singles. These are usually rock stations and are referred to as AOR (album-oriented rock). Distributors seldom send single records to these stations.

Payola

While the system works well for the most part, it is occasionally abused. In the mid 1950s a scandal was exposed that came to be known as "payola." Record distributors were extending their service beyond legal and ethical limits by paying gratuities to stations and disk jockeys for "plugging" certain records. In other words a record was not played because of its artistic merit or the number of requests received for it, but because the disk jockey was accepting favors for playing it. Some well-known personalities were extremely embarrassed when this information was revealed. Charges were brought against the offenders and some heavy fines were imposed. Since then the transactions have been watched closely, and the practice has been largely curtailed.

PROGRAMMING MUSIC

For the majority of stations (both AM and FM) recorded music is the factor most significant in determining the size and characteristics of a station's listening audience. The "sound" of a station refers to the type of music that is played and the sequence of the records. This blend of music can be critical. Just a few records poorly programmed can cause listeners to dial away and perhaps not come back. Program directors are continually seeking reliable data upon which to base their selection of music. Trade magazines, such as *Billboard* and *Cashbox,* provide much information about trends in musical tastes. Record distributors can tell radio stations what albums are selling well and how much promotion is being done on a particular record. Incidentally, it might seem that air play would diminish when a record is owned by a large number of people. But such is apparently not the case. People still call radio stations and request records that they own and can play any time themselves. Some stations rely more heavily upon requests than others. One school of thought is that requests give a more positive indication of the taste of the local community than do the national surveys. Another is that programming on requests is unscientific and may reflect the tastes of only a few listeners. No disk jockey or program director would rely totally upon requests, because there needs to be continuity or flow to the sound of the station. Putting musical selections together in a sequence that is pleasing and harmonious is a talent much like that of a musician. It requires a good ear and a good sense of timing, and should be done by a professional broadcaster rather than a group of casual listeners.

There are numerous surveys taken by a variety of organizations and publications that attempt to identify the most popular musical selections.

One of these is printed out periodically by the Associated Press and distributed to stations over the teletype.

Music Syndicates

The technique of programming music to attract a specific audience segment has in recent years become a science. Companies called *syndicates* are beginning to offer their services to radio stations. Their package includes scientifically programmed music on tape that can be used by a station to obtain a balanced and uniform "sound." The tapes are changed often enough to provide variety and keep up with new moods and trends. This frees the program director from the responsibility and eliminates the need for the disk jockey to spend time selecting music, cuing records, and putting albums back into jackets. He or she can focus full attention upon what is to be said when the microphone is open. Many disk jockeys dislike this system because it deprives them of one of the creative aspects of their business. It also eliminates the possibility of playing requests. Nevertheless, many stations (particularly FM stations) are moving in this direction. It offers several advantages to the station owners. The service provided by syndicates allows a station to operate without a large record library, an extensive filing system, or a music director. The trend may also mean that stations will place more emphasis upon an announcer's ability to talk than to select music.

The Automated Station

Usually the station that subscribes to the syndicated music service is one that is automated. The equipment used by an automated station consists of reel-to-reel tape recorders and banks of cartridge machines that contain the voice tracks (see Figure 8-2). The voice tracks can be spot announcements, ad lib remarks, newscasts, weather reports, or whatever you wish to put on them. They can be changed quickly and easily and programmed to play in any desired sequence. Once the machines have been programmed, they will run automatically, responding to prearranged cues for starting and stopping each tape. Some systems are extremely sophisticated and can even insert time signals. An automated station that is skillfully programmed will sound very much the same as any other station. There may be a lack of flexibility, however, since an automated station cannot play requests. But advocates of automation say that the system provides as much flexibility as most station managements want or need.

Figure 8-2 Automated broadcasting equipment including reel-to-reel tape machines and circular banks of cartridge machines. *(Courtesy Systems Marketing Corporation.)*

PROGRAMMING THE ALL–NEWS STATION

The all-news station is much more difficult and expensive to program than the music station. Generally the personnel is more highly paid and preparation is more extensive. Some stations such as WEEI in Boston and KCBS in San Francisco offer news and talk programs throughout the entire day. This requires the mobilization of many sources of program material. The network and the wire services can provide much of it, but the station staff itself has to generate the most. When WEEI changed from music to news in 1974, they were forced to double their operating budget. Instead of hiring one disk jockey to work a six-hour shift, an all-news station must hire several people who will spend a considerable amount of time writing and doing production work to fill the same amount of air time. News stations require a tremendous amount of copy. WEEI averages twenty-five news stories per hour, plus sports and weather. Some of this will come to the station from the wire services, but much must be written by station personnel. WEEI's full-time news staff increased from eleven people to twenty-eight.

THE TALK SHOW

The talk show is perhaps the most difficult and challenging type of program to do. There are many different formats, but basically they involve talking to people by phone or in person. You will be answering questions as well as asking them and have virtually no time to prepare your responses. Sometimes these talk show hosts or hostesses are called "communicasters." Occasionally they will have source materials on the subject to be discussed, but most of the time they just rely on their knowledge and wits.

The trick is to maintain the interest and attention of the general audience. The communicaster has to maintain a balance between sometimes conflicting responsibilities: that to the person on the phone and a larger one to the listening audience. The caller must not be permitted to go on to the point of boring everyone else. Knowing when and how to terminate the call demands skill, timing, and tact.

There are a number of mechanical aspects characteristic of the talk show that make it complicated. Some radio station insurance contracts insist that there be a 7-second delay between the time the call is received and the time it goes on the air. This allows the engineer time to intercept and delete a remark that might be slanderous or obscene before it can go out over the air. Insurance companies are concerned about this because a station can be sued by an individual slandered by a caller. It can also be fined by the FCC for allowing obscenities on the air.

Technically this delay is accomplished by recording the call on a 7-second cart. The tape moves in a continuous loop and plays back 7 seconds later what it has just recorded. While this solves the problem for the radio station, it often confuses the caller who forgets to turn down the radio. Have you ever tried talking while you were listening to what you said 7 seconds earlier? Even when the program is done without the

7-second delay there are problems. If the caller does not turn down the radio, the sound of the caller's own voice going back into the telephone can cause feedback.

The talk show is normally not a one-person operation. In addition to the communicaster, there is a producer who receives the call first and advises the caller to turn down the radio. The producer can also size up the person on the phone and eliminate the "crank" callers. In order for a talk show to be operated smoothly, there must be at least two in-coming telephone lines. One person should be on "hold" while the communicaster is talking to another. Trying to do talk shows at low-budget stations with only one phone line is awkward. You have to hang up the phone, continue the program by yourself, and wait for the next call to come through. This can be accomplished when you have someone else to talk to, but alone it is very difficult. One variation of the talk show is to have a guest along with the communicaster. Usually the guest is an expert in some field of general interest. The two people can talk together while waiting for calls to come in. However, when there is a call, both people in the studio must be able to hear the person who is on the other end of the wire. For this type of operation you would need what is called a *speaker phone*. This is an instrument that can be provided by the telephone company. It allows the caller's voice to be heard on a small speaker rather than just through the earpiece of the phone. The volume, of course, must be kept very low or it will cause feedback. (The microphones in the studio are open and the communicasters are talking into them.) The speaker phone also allows the caller to hear on the telephone anything that is said by anyone in the room.

Once the technical aspects have been worked out, you can start concentrating on the more important part of the talk show program. What are you going to say? Who will you get as a guest? How can you be sure that people will call? How do you know what to leave in and what to cut out? How do you deal with a caller who will not stop talking? There are a dozen other questions that will come to you when you begin doing it.

Only when you start doing talk shows and interview programs do you begin to realize what modern radio broadcasting is all about and how much you need to know to be successful in the business.

SCHEDULING PROGRAMS

Scheduling the sequence of programs can be done by whim, inspiration, or design. All combinations are possible, but some make more sense than others. You would not insert comedy records in a classical music show; you would not put tragic and humorous stories back-to-back in a newscast; you would not put a commuter report at two o'clock in the afternoon. You may, however, want to program features at a time when other stations are not running them. For example, if every station has news on the hour, you may wish to put yours on the half hour, or 5 minutes before the hour. One good principle to follow is to set consistent times for features, so that people will be able to remember when they are going to occur. Scattering newscasts throughout the day is fine for the person who listens to your station all day long, but not so good for the person who wants to tune in your station to get the news. Timing is important even if you are an independent station and do not have to "hit" a network show. If a newscast is scheduled for three o'clock it should not start 2 minutes before or 2 minutes after. The last record before the newscast can be back-timed so that it will end precisely at three o'clock. There may be listeners who will expect to hear your newscast at the time it is supposed to run. Schedule features and newscasts at times that are logical and easy to remember. Running them on the hour or half hour is the most common practice among the highly professional stations.

Most of your programming may consist of recorded music—the mainstay of modern radio stations. But there will be programs of other types that will be inserted periodically. Remember that the FCC expects you to operate in the public interest. That means you will have to do a certain amount of public affairs programming. This will take the form of documentaries, interviews, panel discussions, phone-in shows, debates, and commentary on current events. These programs should not be regarded as "tune outs." Programs of this sort are often buried, on Sunday morning and at other times when few people are listening, but this ought not to be the rule. There are a number of stations in the country that are quite successful in drawing a listening audience with talk shows. But the programs have to be well done, and they have to be promoted. At some stations disk jockeys are encouraged to ad lib promotional messages for these programs. They may even be given an information sheet that they can use for extemporaneous remarks between records. When a station is involved in a lot of activities, disk jockeys automatically become better informed and have more to talk about. Program directors can facilitate the job of the announcers by providing them with an interesting and dynamic programming schedule.

SUMMARY

Programming is the most important function of a radio station. It is the reason for all of the effort put into transmission. Most commercial broadcasting stations today have discarded the "block programming" concept and think in terms of the overall "sound" rather than individual segments. The program director is the person responsible for producing a consistent and well-balanced sound that will draw listeners and sell the products of the advertisers. A station may choose to become a network affiliate, in which case part of its programming would originate from the network studios in a distant city. The alternative is for the station to be independent and produce its own programming. Most stations rely heavily on recorded music, which is obtained from record distributors. The policy which the station chooses will be a major determinant of the kind of audience the station draws. Some stations may select an all-news format, which is expensive and difficult to produce, but which provides more abundant information and attracts a more mature audience than do other plans.

TERMINOLOGY

Affiliate	Network
AOR	Payola
Block programming	Prime time
Format	Sound
Independent station	Target audience
MOR	Top 40

ACTIVITIES

1 Review the notes you made while you were doing the preparation activities for Chapter 1. What kind of program seems not to be offered in your community? How successful do you think it would be if it were offered? Plan a program of this type. Write an opening and a closing. If it is a musical program, list the selections you would include in the first show of the series. If it is a discussion program, list the participants, the topics to be discussed, and the format you would have the performers follow. Then list suggested content material for other programs in the series.

2 If you have access to audio equipment, produce a pilot program. This will involve getting the records and the people together in a recording studio and putting the program on tape just as it would go on the air.

3 Play the tape for the program director of your college station or one of your community stations. See if you can obtain air time for a series of programs.

Promoting the Station

THE NEED FOR PROMOTION

Promotion is a broad term for advertising. It means providing information about your product and getting people to want to buy it. The product can be a commodity, a service, an idea or concept, an organization, or an individual. In the case of a radio broadcasting station it is the *sound.* "Selling" the product here means getting people to listen, to hear the verbal messages, and to act upon what the announcer is urging them to do. The verbal message may be in the form of poetry, prose, or a musical lyric; the intent of the message may be to inform, remind, or persuade. A broadcasting station can work toward this end by using its own facilities or those of other media, and promotion can attempt to build a listening audience, market the products of advertisers, or acquire new advertising accounts. Let us look at each of these possibilities for promotion in more detail.

BUILDING A LISTENING AUDIENCE

Whether a broadcasting station is commercial or noncommercial, it is interested in building its listening audience. While a noncommercial station may have the support of a philanthropic organization, it still *must* be heard by whatever audience it intends to reach. In the case of a commercial station, listeners are essential for economic survival. When a station attempts to sell its air time, the price is established largely by the size and buying power of the listening audience. In the next chapter we shall talk about measuring the size of the audience, but right now, let us consider ways of building it.

Gimmicks alone cannot build an audience. The station must have an attractive product if it expects to hold onto listeners. We have already discussed some programming concepts that appear to be the determinants of good broadcasting practices. But it is necessary to remember that programming a radio station is not an exact science. Listener behavior is affected not only by the performance of the station, but also by the listener's own individual mood—something over which the station has no control. A particular musical selection may fit in perfectly with a station's format, but might trigger an unhappy recollection in the mind of the listener who would then dial to another station. The best a broadcaster can do is to use good taste and judgment and hope that the listeners will stay, once they have tuned in.

On-the-Air Promotion

The mass media—newspapers, magazines, broadcasting stations—have an advantage over other enterprises: they can promote their product through their own facilities. They can use as much or as little of their own space or air time as they wish. There is, of course, a point of diminishing returns. If a station goes to extremes in using its facilities for promotion, it may have an adverse rather than a positive effect upon the public. Furthermore, the air time of a broadcasting station is not free. The time that is used for promotion could have been drawing revenue from an advertiser. A responsible broadcaster would not want to load up the station with promotional spot announcements, but instead use them with discretion. Most effective is the practice of using promotional spots for calling attention to specific programs or activities of the station.

Promoting Programs   Radio programs can easily be missed. Generally people do not look in the paper for specific radio programs as they do for television programs. Seldom are programs rerun, unless they are exceptionally good. So it is important that, somehow, you let people know when you are going to do something special. The best way is to promote the program on your own station. The motto of good promotion is *Plan Ahead.* Do not let things just happen without giving notice in advance that they are going to happen. You may put many hours of work into a program and have only a few listeners, because you failed to promote it. Modesty is not called for when you think you have something good. Advertise it!

A promotional spot in radio is called a *promo.* It tells the listener what to listen for and when to listen:

> Next Tuesday night KFJC will cover the election returns. Our reports will begin at 8 o'clock when the polls close and continue until a definite trend has been established. We'll have reports direct from the county election office, interviews with the candidates, and the results of a study conducted by De Anza College on the voting habits of college students. It all happens next Tuesday night right here on KFJC.

You might want to make a production spot out of this, with music and sound effects in the background. Notice that the important information has been repeated just as it is in any other commercial or public service announcement. Promos are scheduled into the log like any other spot. Usually they are logged as SP (station promo) or SC (station continuity), rather than as COM (commercial) or PSA (public service announcement).

Institutional Promotion   Another type of promotion advertises the station in general rather than a specific program. This is known as *institutional promotion,* and its purpose is to fix the name of a company or product in the public mind. Even if people do not listen to a station, it is advantageous for it to be recognized—if possible, to become a "household word." People all over the country have heard of *The New York Times,* even if most of them have never read it. Few radio stations are likely to achieve such nationwide reputations, but some are better known than others. KSFO used to bill itself as "The world's greatest radio station—especially in San Francisco." While they may not have had the highest rating in the area, everyone was familiar with their call letters.

Call letters can be a significant factor contributing to the individuality and identity of a station. The selection of call letters is subject to the approval of the FCC. There are certain criteria that must be met: One is that all stations east of the Mississippi begin with W and those to the west with K. Another is that there must be no two alike. A third, of course, is that the combination of letters must be in good taste—the FCC would not permit obscene or suggestive words. Within these limitations, stations try to pick for themselves call letters that are easily remembered and pertain in some way to their region, local environment, affiliation, or style of programming. Examples would be KCBS, the CBS affiliate in San Francisco; KJAZ, which programs jazz music; and KGMS, the good music station in Sacramento. Our own station in Los Altos Hills uses the call letters KFJC, standing for Foothill Junior College. When we became known as a Community College, we considered changing our call letters to KFCC, but we were afraid the Commission would not approve.

The main purpose of call letters is to provide clear identification of a broadcasting station. The FCC requires that this identification be made at least every hour, but it does not set a maximum number of times that the call letters can be used. Some stations make a policy of using the call letters frequently so that the audience always knows what station it is listening to. But overusage does tend to get tiresome, especially when the call letters are attached to time, weather, newsbriefs, and almost every other statement an announcer is likely to make. Some stations prefer to focus attention upon their frequency rather than the call letters, on the theory that it is important for the listener to know the location of the station on the dial. Both frequency and call letters can be promoted in a variety of ways. Pronouncing the combination of letters as a word is one of the more common methods. For example, KABL becomes "cable." In other cases, stations will use rhyming words or slogans. Perhaps the most popular course of all is to incorporate the call letters into a musical jingle. One station in San Francisco used a clever device to associate the call letters with the frequency. Their position on the FM dial is 101 megahertz and they selected the call letters of KIOI. They identify themselves unofficially as kay-one-oh-one. Their legal identification on the hour, of course, still must be KIOI.

Promoting Personalities   A station may or may not wish to invest heavily in the promotion of their on-the-air personnel. Some that do are well rewarded. As the fortunes of the personality rise, so do those of the station. It is certainly to the advantage of a station to employ a popular disk jockey whom everyone wants to listen to. The disadvantage is that the personality becomes very expensive and often is wooed by other stations. Some disk jockeys have the power to command large audiences and possess the ability to retain their listeners even when they move to a new station. Before a station makes a big investment in any one employee, it must be certain to have the individual under a strong contract. One such disk jockey, Don Sherwood, had to agree that when he left KSFO, he would not go to work for any other radio station in the San Francisco Bay area.

Some disk jockeys try to do their own promotion. However, a radio personality of purely local standing has limited resources in this direction. Since networks do not carry disk jockey programs, there is no chance of obtaining nationwide recognition. Also fan clubs are rare for the D.J. But there are other things radio personalities can do for their own promotion. Sometimes they will have made, at their own expense, their own musical jingles and signatures. D.J.'s who pay for these productions themselves will probably not include the station call letters in them. The jingle is the performer's own property and can be taken along to another station.

Another opportunity for the enterprising D.J. is to make personal appearances. The qualities of a good disk jockey generally include those of a good master of ceremonies. Stations like to have their air personalities go out into the community to be the host or hostess on ceremonial occasions. Sometimes the D.J. can pick up extra money by playing records at dances and discos. These kinds of opportunities are available in the small, rural communities as well as in the larger metropolitan areas. Often small, local stations will sponsor dances and perhaps even broadcast the Firemen's Ball or the Grange Hall Social.

The station can profit from the popularity of a disk jockey. It is always good for a station to increase the size of its listening audience. But more directly, the popular D.J. can attract sponsors. A D.J. with a unique and appealing style may be sought by local merchants to do their commercials. The merchant may request that the D.J. do the announcement live and give it a special treatment. In this case the advantage is to the station rather than to the D.J. On other occasions the merchant may request that the spot be recorded so that it can be used on other stations. Under these circumstances the D.J. would receive a *talent fee*. This fee can range from just a few dollars to a considerable sum. If the spot announcement is to run often and on a number of different stations, the announcer's contract may provide for *residuals*. Residuals are fees paid to the performers on a recording based on the number of times it is played on the air. An announcer who becomes well known in the broadcasting industry can make a good living working for national accounts.

Contests   One method of building an audience commonly used by radio stations is to hold contests. This method is controversial and shunned by many station managers, because it is expensive and does not always produce lasting results. The propriety of using contests to gain listeners is also questionable. Some consider it to be tantamount to bribery or pandering. Supporters of contests, however, regard them as effective in merchandising products as well as increasing the size of a listening audience. A contest may draw listeners to a station and hold them until the payoff. But it is the quality of the station's regular programming that will ultimately determine its rating.

Any contest must, of course, be conducted within the legal limits set by the FCC and state and federal statutes.[1] In order to avoid being classified as a lottery, a contest must meet certain criteria. The contest may offer prizes of cash or merchandise; it may be based upon chance; but it must not require monetary consideration of the participants. In other words, neither the station nor the sponsoring merchant may require any fee or purchase of tickets or merchandise as a condition of eligibility to win. Qualifications, such as age, may be imposed, but there must not be entry fees of any kind. A merchant can require that contestants come into the store for application blanks but, again, may not require purchases.

Most radio contests require that participants call or write the station. This draws attention to the station and also serves as a monitoring device for estimating numbers of listeners. In addition, it provides the station with a mailing list that can be used for future promotional campaigns.

The chief expense of a contest is the cost of the prizes. A station can offset this cost by giving advertising time to the contributors of prizes. Here again, the station must weigh the value of its own air time. The spot announcement that is used for promoting the donor of a prize constitutes revenue lost to the station. A station may want to utilize its own facilities to defray expenses, but not to its own detriment.

MARKETING THE ADVERTISER'S PRODUCT

Building a large listening audience is only one part of the goal of a commercial radio station. Another is marketing the products of the advertisers. The two are often related, but they are not identical. A message may be heard by a great many people, but unless the listeners buy the product, the advertiser is wasting money. It is entirely possible that a participating sponsor may be selling a product that does not appeal to the radio station's listeners. For example, banks and insurance companies may not be helped by advertising on a rock and roll station, regardless of the number of listeners it may have. From a marketing point of view, the station with a smaller, more affluent audience may produce better results. A commercial station needs to get results for its advertisers; just reading the messages on the air is not enough. That is why stations offer other marketing services in addition to spot announcements.

[1] See Chapter 3, page 25.

Off-The-Air Promotion

The broadcasters that are most successful commercially are those that consider themselves to be in the merchandising business, rather than in the entertainment business. Off-the-air promotion can be good for the station and for the sponsor as well. Bumper stickers are commonly used by radio stations as promotional devices. The stickers give the call letters of the station and perhaps a slogan for further identification. As an incentive for people to put stickers on their cars, the station and/or the sponsor may offer added benefits. A sponsor may give a discount, for example, to customers who have certain stickers or identifying symbols on their cars. Sometimes the station itself will give prizes to motorists selected at random who are displaying the stickers.

A practice that is gaining increasing support is to pass the cost of promotion on to the consumer. There was a time when advertisements had to be given away, and people had to be paid to display them. No longer. The public is quite willing to buy tee shirts, beer mugs, book covers, ice chests, and a variety of other items that display advertising logos, not just at cost, but at a profit to the manufacturer. All over the country people are volunteering to become walking billboards and are willing to pay for the privilege.

Trips with D.J.s   A promotional device that is popular with disk jockeys is for them to take trips with listeners. Both the D.J. and the listeners who are selected get expense-paid weekends to some vacation resort. This is an expensive operation for the station, but it has proven to be successful in gaining and holding listeners. The attraction is that people have to listen to the station in order to win. They must hear their names mentioned on the air and must call in within a certain period of time. The vacation provides the added dimension of establishing a very close rapport between the listener and the radio station. The individual who gets to know a D.J. personally is going to become an avid fan. The trip may be financed by the radio station for the sake of obtaining listeners, or it may have the backing of a commercial enterprise. Airlines or travel agencies, for example, may wish to sponsor such an endeavor, or at least share the expenses with the broadcaster. Often the arrangements are made by an advertising agency, which works out all the details and sells the "package" to a station and a sponsor, jointly.

Trade-outs   In broadcasting not all business is conducted on a cash basis. Occasionally the barter system is used. A trade-out is just such an arrangement. A station may run spot announcements for a company and receive a product or a service in exchange. It is not uncommon for resorts and hotels to contract for advertising time and then make accommodations available to employees of the radio station. This practice must, of course, be done through the sales department of the station. It is illegal for station personnel to make their own private arrangements with commercial enterprises and receive favors, without having such transactions cleared through the accounting department. This type of under-the-table operation is referred to as "payola" and is a violation of federal law.[2]

ACQUIRING NEW ACCOUNTS

Marketing a sponsor's product means, in the first place, acquiring the advertiser's business. It is not sufficient for a station to provide quality programming and gain large numbers of listeners; the broadcaster must also make these facts known to those who are in the business of buying air time. Local sales representatives will carry the word to the local merchants; national representatives will make it known to the larger accounts. But to broaden the scope of coverage, radio stations often advertise in periodicals. The most widely read magazines are those with national circulation. But, of course, a local broadcasting station does not need national coverage. To accommodate local and regional advertisers, magazines such as *Time, Newsweek,* and *Sports Illustrated* offer special rates for limited coverage. The advertisement will appear only in those copies of the periodical which are distributed in one or another particular part of the country. (In other words, each issue of the magazine is made up in several different versions.) In this way broadcasters can get the attention, not only of advertising agencies, but of potential listeners as well, without the enormous expense of unneeded coverage. To sharpen the focus of the promotion campaign, the broadcaster will also advertise in the *trade journals.* A trade journal is a magazine published for the benefit of the people in a particular industry or profession. For radio and television the most widely distributed trade magazine is *Broadcasting,* which is published weekly and distributed nationwide. In most states there are other trade publications serving the local regions. They are valuable assets to broadcasters because they are read by advertisers as well as by people in the radio and television profession.

PROFESSIONAL ASSOCIATIONS

In addition to trade journals, broadcasting stations that try to maintain a high degree of professionalism actively support and call upon their *professional associations.* These are organizations which can provide considerable help in feeding information to broadcasters and looking out for

[2] See Chapter 8, page 96.

their interests. The most influencial broadcasting organization in this country is the National Association of Broadcasters (NAB), which has been instrumental in formulating public policy as it pertains to the broadcasting industry. While NAB is open to anyone, it is primarily an organization for commercial broadcasters. Noncommercial stations are represented by CPB—the Corporation for Public Broadcasting. This is a private, nonprofit corporation, established to foster the growth and development of the nation's noncommercial radio and television stations. College stations have their own association, the Intercollegiate Broadcasting System (IBS), which has been extremely helpful in aiding in the establishment and development of college radio.[3] In addition to the associations mentioned above, there are numerous local and regional organizations to which broadcasters can turn for advice and assistance. The promotion of the industry as a whole may not be felt at the grass roots level immediately, but in the long run it has been largely responsible for the success that radio and television stations enjoy.

SUMMARY

Promotion is important to a radio station. It means developing the influence of a station by building a listening audience and helping sponsors to sell their products. Stations are continually trying to get people to listen. They do this by improving their programming and by thinking of gimmicks to gain and hold the attention of listeners. Contests are successful in doing this, but may not have long-lasting effects. Individual disk jockeys advance their own fortunes as well as the stations' for which they work by extending themselves to the community. They can also pick up extra money by doing commercials for large advertisers. A radio station can promote its own cause by utilizing other media in addition to its own facilities. Bumper stickers and tee shirts are common devices and popular among listeners. Broadcasters often use periodicals for advertising their stations, particularly the trade journals. Radio and television stations also rely on professional organizations to promote and enhance the industry as a whole.

TERMINOLOGY

    Corporation for Public Broadcasting (CPB)
    Institutional promotion
    Intercollegiate Broadcasting System (IBS)
    National Association of Broadcasters (NAB)

---

[3] Membership information for IBS can be obtained by writing to Intercollegiate Broadcasting System, Inc., Box 592, Vails Gate, New York 12584.

Promotion spot
Promo
Residuals
Station continuity (SC)
Station promo (SP)
Talent fee
Trade journal
Trade-outs

ACTIVITIES

1 Plan a contest suitable for a radio station promotional campaign. Be realistic about the prizes to be given away. Plan all aspects of the contest. Consider the qualifications of the contestants, what they need to do to win, how their entries will be judged, how the prizes will be awarded to the winners, and how the station will announce the winners. If the contest involves a quiz, write the questions and answers. If it is a puzzle, be sure it is not too hard or too easy. You want some winners, but not too many. Estimate how many people would be interested in such a contest and how many listeners the station could expect to draw.

2 Write a promotional spot announcement for the contest. Give enough information so that people will be able to understand what it is about. Be sure to tell when it starts and who is eligible.

3 Go to the library and get a copy of one of the professional journals or broadcasting trade magazines. See what advertisements the periodical contains. Are the advertisements directed to the listener or to the sponsor? See what other information there is in the magazine that might be useful to the radio broadcaster.

Financing the Station

SOURCES OF INCOME

Every month somebody has to pay the bills. This is true for a radio station, just as it is for any other business enterprise. There is a payroll to meet, rent to be paid, equipment to be repaired, materials to be purchased, and numerous other expenses. A radio station is expensive to operate, and it must have a substantial source of income. Let us look at some of the ways a station might sustain itself.

A station may be *commercial* or *noncommercial*. If it is licensed as a commercial station it is permitted to sell advertising time. It can sell the time in "blocks" of 30 minutes or an hour; or it can sell short spot announcements. Most stations choose to sell their time in short spots of 30 seconds or a minute. These spot announcements are distributed throughout the broadcast day. Commercial stations employ sales representatives to find advertisers who wish to buy time on the station. The person performing this job may be a *local time* salesperson, or a *national representative.* The local time salesperson deals with the merchants of the local community; the national representative handles the big accounts that are advertised nationally. Sales is one of the most important aspects of commercial operation.

A noncommercial station is not permitted to sell advertising. The terms of the license specifically state that money can not be received for the endorsement of a commerical product. The noncommercial station must therefore find other ways to obtain the income that is required for day-to-day operation. In this chapter we will look in some detail at the means of financing both commercial and noncommercial stations.

COMMERCIAL STATIONS

Most broadcasting stations are commercial and financed by revenue received from advertisers who buy air time. In the early days of radio this air time was available in "blocks" consisting of 5-, 10-, 15-, 30-, and 60-minute segments. Sponsors would buy blocks of time and produce their own programs to fit. The programs were often carried on a network and featured big-name personalities. In between the programs, stations would run short "spot" announcements, sometimes called "station break" or "chain break" spots. The demise of "block" programming was the result of several factors: television consumed almost all of the big-name drama and comedy programs; independent stations (not affiliated with networks) began to spring up; radio went to a music-news format; and station owners saw the value of maintaining a consistent "sound" throughout the day, rather than jumping from one type of program to another. So it is now the local radio station owner, rather than the advertiser, who determines the content of the programming. Sponsors who wish to buy time have control of the material in their advertisement, but that is all. They may write the copy and have it produced by an outside agency, but they have little if any say over the program into which it is inserted. A station owner may make an effort to accommodate an advertiser who wants to sign a long-term contract but has to take into consideration the other sponsors who may also be buying time in the same segment. What is more, the broadcaster must also be in touch with the listeners' tastes and desires. A station does not gain much if it wins a sponsor but loses the audience.

THE SALES STAFF

Your chances of breaking into the profession of broadcasting are good if you have the ability to sell. All too often students overlook this aspect of the business, when actually it is the most promising. Not only will you earn more money as a salesperson than as a disk jockey, but the hours will be better too. The person who has the best chance of being hired is the one who can do a combination of things. If you can write copy, operate the equipment so that you can record your own spots, announce, and also bring in accounts, you can be a very valuable member of any radio broadcasting staff.

Your success as a salesperson will be determined by a number of factors: the popularity of the station, the number of people who listen, the ratings, the promotion campaigns, the type of programming offered, the quality of the announcers, and of course, the cost of the spot announcements.

The Local Sales Representative

Every commercial station has a sales staff headed by a *sales manager.* The number of sales personnel employed will depend upon the size of the station and the size of the community. Usually the salesperson works on a commission basis, earning approximately 15 percent of the "billing." Often the people in the sales department are the highest-paid members of the staff. The local sales representative contacts the merchants in the community and tries to persuade them to buy spot announcements. He or she will try to get them on a long-term contract if possible by pointing out that the cost per spot is less if the maximum is purchased. (See the Rate Card.) Personality characteristics and techniques used by the radio time salesperson are similar to those found in any other area of selling.

The National Representative

In addition to the local accounts, radio stations need to obtain business from large, national advertisers. To do this, it is necessary to have contacts in all the major cities, and normally a small, local station would not have sufficient money or resources. So, to acquire the large accounts, a station will contract with a *national representative.* This is a company that specializes in acquiring for local stations the big national accounts. A *national rep* will deal with the agencies that handle the advertising for products distributed nationwide. This is something you may want to take into consideration if you plan to apply for a job as a salesperson. Much of the advertising that is done by stations in large metropolitan markets is handled by the national reps. Therefore, the local time salesperson in a major market may not have as much opportunity as the sales representative in a smaller market.

THE RATE CARD

Suppose you are the one who determines the cost of each spot announce-ment. How are you going to know what to charge? A simple answer would be "whatever the traffic will bear," and that would not be far wrong. Your rate might be determined by what an advertiser is willing to pay, but it might also reflect your cost of operation. To compute this, take your total cost of operation for a full year. That would include salaries, rent, taxes, depreciation on equipment, maintenance, office sup-plies, promotion costs, lawyers' fees, custodial service—everything. Di-vide that by 365 to get the cost of operation for one day. Then decide how many spot announcements you want to run per day. You may be tempted to say, "as many as I can sell." For a number of reasons, unfor-tunately, you cannot use that as a guide. First, because the National Association of Broadcasters' *Radio Code* specifies that there shall be no more than 18 minutes of commercial time per hour. And the FCC will expect you to abide by that. Second, because the number of spots you sell will depend to a large extent upon how much you charge for each one. And third, because your listening audience will diminish if you run too many commercials. So you have some choices to make. You can keep your operating costs down so that you could afford to run few commercials in an effort to build your listening audience. As you do that, you will gradually be able to increase the cost of each spot. If it turns out that your station is not taking in enough revenue to meet expenses, you must either cut your overhead, increase the cost of your spot announcements, or sell more of them. Suppose you need to earn $800 a day to meet all of your expenses. If you wanted to run two hundred spots per day, you could sell them for only four dollars. But you would probably want to run only one hundred per day and sell them for eight dollars. Better still, run only fifty and sell each one for sixteen dollars.

Consider too, that during some hours of the day you will have more listeners than at others. You will be able to charge more for the spots that run during peak traffic periods. Most stations divide the day into two or three *classes* and charge premium rates for high priority times. The *length* of the spot will also affect the cost. Most spots are either 30 seconds or a minute; occasionally there will be 15-second spots too. In addition, a station may offer a *frequency discount.* This means that the more spots an advertiser contracts for, the smaller the cost per spot. All of this may sound very confusing, so in order to make it understandable to a potential advertiser, a station will print what it calls a *rate card.* A typical one is shown in Figure 10-1.

The rate card is easy enough to read. If the sponsor buys five 60-

```
                         WEEKLY RATES
                       One-minute Spots

   Class "AA" TIME (6 to 10 A.M. and 3 to 7 P.M. . . . Monday through Friday)

   Spots per
   week      1 to 3 weeks   4 to 12 weeks   13 to 25 weeks   26 to 52 weeks

     5          $27.50         $23.00          $20.75           $16.50

    10           26.00          21.50           19.25            15.50

    15           24.50          20.50           18.50            14.50

   CLASS "A" TIME (All other times except midnight to 5 A.M.)

   Spots per
   week      1 to 3 weeks   4 to 12 weeks   13 to 25 weeks   26 to 52 weeks

     5          $19.50         $16.00          $14.50           $11.50

    10           18.50          15.50           14.00            11.00

    15           18.00          15.00           13.50            10.50

   CLASS "B" TIME (Midnight to 5 A.M.) = 1/2 of applicable class "A" rate
```

Figure 10-1 Rate card.

second spots to be run in 1 to 3 weeks during class AA time, the cost is $27.50 per spot. At fifteen spots per week over a 52-week period, the same spot costs only $14.50. Advertisers know that buying as few as five radio spots does practically no good at all; announcements must be purchased in some quantity in order to be effective. Generally a sponsor will select one or more stations which reach the audience desired and run several spots a day over a long period of time. Occasionally the sponsor will have a big event, such as a sale or the introduction of a new product, and will want to *saturate* the market for just a few days. For these occasions a station may offer the sponsor *saturation packages* (see Figure 10-2).

The rate card may also include a map showing the station's area of coverage. With 50,000 watts this San Jose station shown in Figure 10-3 gets good coverage of the South San Francisco Bay Region.

But how does an advertiser know what station to buy? And how do you, as an advertising salesperson, let your client know that your station will do some good? You have little that is tangible when you are selling air time. The advertiser could use the trial-and-error method, but it is difficult to know whether or not the announcement running on *your* station is bringing in any business. From time to time customers may say that they heard an announcement on the radio, but that is not a reliable index. Holding contests or making special offers to radio listeners is another method of gauging response, but a company would not want to do that all the time. An advertiser may rely upon personal taste and

```
                        SATURATION PACKAGES

3-Day Saturation/Sun.-Mon.-Tues. Only
──────────────
30 Announcements (Minutes = $300.00 and 30 Seconds = $240.00)
Announcements will be scheduled as evenly as possible in all day parts.
(Best Times Available, 6 A.M. to Midnight)

5-Day Saturation/Mon. thru Fri.
──────────────
50 Announcements (Minutes = $550.00 and 30 Seconds = $440.00)
Announcements will be scheduled as evenly as possible in all day parts
(BTA).

7-Day Saturation/Mon. thru Sun.
──────────────
70 Announcements (Minutes = $700.00 and 30 Seconds = $560.00)
Announcements will be scheduled as evenly as possible in all day parts
(BTA).
```

Figure 10-2 Saturation package.

instinct, but that is a bit unscientific. To a large extent, salespersons will be selling their energy, creativeness, and concern for clients. They will *service* their accounts regularly—that is, call upon clients often and make sure that the commercial copy is up to date. Advertisers do not like to be forgotten about once they have signed contracts. A salesperson knows that in order to keep an account, the client must believe that the advertisements are doing some good.

AUDIENCE SURVEY REPORTS

The most reliable evidence that a salesperson has to work with are audience survey reports. These do not tell the advertiser how many customers a spot announcement is bringing, but they do show how many people were exposed to the message. Moreover, the survey will show the *demographics*[1] of the audience. Age and sex are the two factors that seem to be the most significant. An advertiser may be interested in reaching a male audience between 18 and 25, and so, will select a station which attracts that particular segment of listeners.

One of the most widely used audience survey reports is Arbitron Radio. It collects its data by issuing diaries to a carefully selected cross section of a given population. The people who agree to keep the diaries record their radio listening in quarter-hour segments for a period of several weeks. The returns are assembled, published, and distributed to broadcasting stations which have contracted for the service. The "Book"

---

[1] Demographics are sociological characteristics that include ethnic background, economic status, religious affiliation, and many other factors in addition to age and sex.

COVERAGE MAP

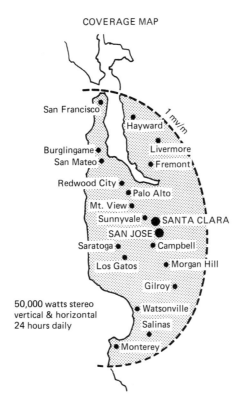

Figure 10-3 Coverage map. *(Courtesy KARA.)*

is expensive, but it is valuable to the broadcaster. It provides evidence that can be shown to sponsors to demonstrate the effectiveness of the station. Even stations that are low in the report can use the survey to their advantage. For example, the low-rated station can show that it charges less for its spot announcements and has a lower cost per listener than its competitor. Other stations may take pride in the fact that they have the highest ratings in a particular time period or for a particular audience segment. This may be more important than the overall *cumulative* rating.

Rating and Share

In looking at audience survey reports you must distinguish between the *rating* and the *share*. To compute a rating, you need two numbers: the total population and the number of people who have listened to a particular station.

$$\frac{\text{Number of listeners}}{\text{Total population}} = \text{rating (\%)}$$

There are two kinds of ratings. *Average-quarter-hour* ratings tell you what percentage of the total population was listening during an average quarter hour in a given time period. *Cumulative* ratings tell you what percentage of the total population listened at least once during the time period measured. In other words one person may have listened to 8 quarter hours of one station over a 4-hour period. The average-quarter-hour persons for the 4-hour period would be *one half* of a listener because there are 16 quarter hours in a 4-hour period. Each quarter hour is counted separately; the person would have to have listened in all of the quarter-hour segments to be counted as one full listener. If one person represents five hundred in the survey, (one person contacted out of every five hundred) the formula would be:

$$(500 \times 8 \text{ quarter hours}) \div 16 = 250 \text{ average-quarter-hour persons}$$

This would then be divided by the total population to give the *average-quarter-hour* rating. If there are 10,000 people in the total population, the formula would be:

$$\frac{250}{10,000} = 0.025 \text{ or an average-quarter-hour rating of } 2.5\%$$

Now let's look at *cumulative* ratings. In this case each person is counted only once for listening at any time during the 4-hour period. So the cumulative ratings will be higher even though the number of listeners is the same. Again, consider the one person who represents 500 in our survey. If that person listened at any time during the 4-hour period we compute the cumulative ratings as follows:

$$\frac{500}{10,000} = 0.05 \text{ or a cumulative rating of } 5\%$$

It is understandable why stations prefer to talk in terms of "cume" (cumulative) ratings rather than average-quarter-hour ratings.

The *share* of the audience is the ratio of the number of listeners to the number of stations to which they were listening. Or, another way of saying it: *share* is the average number of persons who listen to a station during a given quarter hour, expressed as a percentage of all persons who listened to radio during the time period measured. To calculate *share* you need two numbers: the total listening audience during a particular quarter-hour segment, and the number of people listening to a particular station in that quarter-hour segment.

$$\frac{\text{Number of people listening to a particular station}}{\text{Total number of people listening to all stations}} = \text{share of audience for a particular station}$$

It is important to distinguish between *share* and *rating*. Both are shown in percent, but they should not be confused or interchanged. Remember that rating always relates to the total population, whereas audience share is the percentage of people listening to the radio. Let's say, for example, that a station has a ten percent share of the audience in the morning, and a twenty percent share at night. This means that the station is doing better at night in comparison to other stations even though there may be more people listening in the morning hours. The ratings for all stations may go down, but you are in good shape if your share of the audience continues to be high. The rating is important to advertisers, though, because it tells them how many people their messages are reaching. In this way they can calculate how much it is costing them to reach each listener.

NONCOMMERCIAL STATIONS

A noncommercial station is one that may not receive payment for advertising goods and services. It is issued a license by the Federal Communications Commission specifically stating that no charge may be made for the promotion or endorsement of commercial products. Usually people operate these stations for reasons other than the profit motive. They may feel, for example, that the cultural enrichment of the community is not being provided by the commercial stations. They may wish to offer certain types of programming, such as drama or classical music, which are often not scheduled by the commercial stations. The reason may also be to provide broadcasting experience for those wishing to enter the field. But whatever their reasons may be, they have to have some means of raising revenue other than selling commercials. There are several possibilities open to them.

Listener Support   There are several radio and television stations in this country that are supported primarily by money contributed by listeners. This is a tenuous means of financing a station. It requires broad coverage and loyal listeners. Stations that use this method sometimes find themselves in a dilemma. Their main purpose is to provide alternative programming (that which appeals to a minority of listeners), but at the same time they must attract an audience large enough to provide adequate support. In addition they must devote a certain amount of their air time to making appeals for money which in some cases can be as offensive as commercials.

Corporation for Public Broadcasting   This is a private, nonprofit corporation that was established to implement the Public Broadcasting Act of 1967. Through government and private financing, it makes funds available to noncommercial radio and television stations. CPB does not directly produce radio programs, but it does provide grants to stations for various purposes. It helps new stations get on the air and assists in the expansion of existing ones. A radio station would not rely totally upon CPB for support; it would look for other means of financing as well.

National Public Radio   Stations which are eligible for CPB funding may receive and broadcast programs produced by National Public Radio. NPR has extensive resources to which a local station would not have access. This provides a means for noncommercial stations to compete in quality and coverage with the large commercial networks.

Institutional Support   Many noncommercial stations are financed by institutions such as schools and churches. Just like all other stations, they must abide by the rules of the Fairness Doctrine and not espouse their cause to the exclusion of others. They are useful in providing their parent institutions with a voice to publicize important messages and activities. Colleges often support broadcasting stations for the purpose of offering a training ground for students and a means of reaching a large segment of the community. A station funded by an institution is relieved of the need to make appeals to the public for donations.

Underwriting   This is a method of financing available to all noncommercial stations. It permits the broadcaster to mention the name of a commercial organization that has provided funding for the support of the station. This is allowed under FCC *Rules and Regulations* as long as certain criteria are met.[2] No product may be *endorsed* by the station; you

[2] FCC *Rules and Regulations,* 73:503.

may not urge people to buy from, or even visit, any establishment. You may give only the *name* of the company—not its address, phone number, or even a description of its merchandise. The announcement may appear once at the beginning and once at the end of the program. Usually it is phrased in the following manner: "This program is made possible through a grant from the _____ corporation."

Public radio and television stations can make good use of this method of financing. Companies are, of course, allowed to deduct the donation from their income taxes, and in addition they get their names out to the public. Underwriting is popular among large corporations eager to improve their public image and to let people know they are supporting community affairs.

SUMMARY

Every station needs to be financed in some way. Most commercial stations are able to make a substantial profit by selling advertisements. The young person thinking of going into the broadcasting field should seriously consider radio sales; salaries and commissions are higher in that area than in any other area of broadcasting. The amount that a station can charge for its spot announcements is closely related to the number of listeners it has. In the metropolitan areas, stations compete fiercely for high ratings. The higher the rating the more a station can charge for its announcements, and the better the chance the salesperson has to sell air time. Noncommercial stations do not have to compete in the "numbers game." They are not under as much pressure, but they also are generally forced to operate on much smaller budgets.

TERMINOLOGY

Average-quarter-hour ratings
Book
Block programming
Chain break spots
Class A time
CPB (Corporation for Public Broadcasting)
Cumes (cumulative ratings)
Demographics
Frequency discount
Fringe area
National representative (national rep)
NPR (National Public Radio)
Rate card
Rating

Saturation
Share
Underwriting

ACTIVITIES

1 Contact a commercial station in your local area and ask to see the rate card. Talk with the sales manager and ask how long the rates have been in effect and what makes them go up or down. Specifically, ask how much the survey reports affect the station's rates. Ask if you can see a copy of the most recent ratings, and see how the station stands in popularity compared to the other stations in the area. Find out what the station considers to be its strongest selling point.

2 Contact a noncommercial station and ask if they have an underwriting program. If so, find out how they obtain contributors and how much of the station's total revenue is provided by underwriting contracts.

3 There are 300,000 people in a station's listening radius. A survey company contacted 1,000 people, so each contact represents 300 people. One hundred of them said they had listened to a particular station at least once during a 4-hour period. What is the station's cumulative rating during that period? Those same 100 people said they listened to 6 of the 16 quarter hours in that time period. What is the average-quarter-hour rating for that time period?

4 Count the number of commercials during prime time on an AM radio station. Compare that to the number of commercials during prime time on an FM station.

Chapter 11

Writing for Radio

THE COPYWRITER

Consider the amount of copy that is consumed by a radio station. Let's
say a station is on the air 24 hours a day and has a 5-minute newscast
every hour for a total of 120 minutes of news. If there is an average of ten
spot announcements per hour, you have another 240 minutes of talk, for
a total of 360 minutes per day. The normal reading speed for most announcers is about 160 words per minute. Multiply that out and you get
57,600 words of copy that have to be read every broadcast day—as many
words as there are in a good-size novel. Who writes all that copy? Well,
much of it is repetitious; the same spot announcement is read many
times over. Most of the news comes from the wire services and other
agencies to which the station might subscribe. But a good deal of the
copy is written by employees of the station itself. A large station may
employ several writers just for the news department. There may be
others who write commercial copy and public service announcements.

125

At smaller stations, the writing is done by combo operators and sales personnel. The ability to write is definitely an asset to any employee of a radio station. Writing means being able to type, as well as construct sentences and develop paragraphs. If you have this ability, be sure to put it down on your résumé when you are applying for a job. In this chapter we shall take up the kind of writing you would do as an employee of a station. We shall also consider the writing you might want to do as a private citizen to gain access to the airwaves and to gain experience in preparing for a career in broadcasting.

PREPARING COMMERCIAL COPY

For the commercial radio station, spot announcements are the primary source of revenue. The station can stay in business only as long as it can sell the products of its advertisers through commercial announcements. Some of the copy for these announcements is received directly from advertising departments and agencies. But much of it is written by personnel of the radio station. Often the salesperson will write the copy for his or her own account. This is a logical procedure because the salesperson is the one in closest contact with the advertiser and has the best idea of what needs to be said in the copy. The conscientious salesperson will make regular calls on the account to see what new information should be included. To be effective in sales, you have to keep in continuous contact with the advertiser and make sure the copy is updated. This is called "servicing the account" and is a necessary responsibility of the salesperson.

Length

The typical spot announcement is precisely one minute in length—about 160 words at the average speaking rate. The cost of a spot announcement is determined, in part, by its duration. If a sponsor is paying for a full minute of air time, the copywriter should be sure that the sponsor gets it. But the station does not want to give time that is not paid for. So length is an important factor. The reading time of the spot should be specified at the top of the copy. The usual time units of less than one minute are 10, 15, 20, or 30 seconds.

Information

Information for the copy will be obtained from the sponsor or by an agent of the sponsor. Be sure you get it accurately. After you have written the spot, have it approved by the sponsor. Remember that both the advertiser and you are responsible for what is said on the air. If you get the price wrong on a sale item, the advertiser has to sell the product at that price. If there is a major discrepancy, the radio station could be sued for the difference. It would be a good idea for you to become acquainted with the laws covering truth in advertising.

Spot announcements should include some specific information. Slogans and platitudes do reinforce recognition of the sponsor's name, but do not motivate the consumer to purchase the product. Your job as a copywriter is to provide some reason to make the listener at least want to go into the store and look at the product. You have to make the product sound unique in some way, so that it is more desirable than other products of the same type. The difference could be the price, a feature of the product itself, the convenience of shopping, the attractiveness of the surroundings, the pleasure or excitement the product will bring, the friends or lovers that will be attracted by it, or the degree to which it will improve the purchaser's marriage, career, or golf score.

While the information should be specific, do not overload the listener with too much detail. Remember, the listener is probably not taking notes as you talk. If you give the address, do not give the telephone number; that would be too many numbers to keep in mind. The information you want the listener to retain should go at the end of the copy.

Form and Style

The copy should be typewritten and double-spaced. Words should be spelled correctly so that the reader will be able to make them out. Sentences should be fairly short, and punctuation should contribute to readability. Remember that the punctuation can not be seen by the listener; it is there only for the sake of facilitating the interpretation the reader gives to the copy. Underline words or phrases that you want emphasized or stressed. The heading for the copy should contain three important pieces of information:

1   The reading time.
2   The name of the sponsor who is paying for the announcement. If it is a public service announcement, enter the name of the organization which is taking responsibility for the message.
3   The "kill" date. This is the date and time the announcement should no longer be aired. If there is no kill date, put the letters "TFN," which stand for "till further notice."

The name of the sponsor should be clearly stated so that the traffic director knows how to log the announcement, and so that the accounting department knows who gets the bill. It is also required by the Federal

Communications Commission that each announcement contain the name of the sponsor. The public has a right to know who stands to gain as a result of their responding to the message. Taking all of these factors into account, here is what a typical 30-second commercial spot announcement would look like.

Kelly's Hardware

30 seconds

Kill: September 3rd

This week Kelly's Hardware puts the accent on insulation. If your house has been uncomfortably *hot* this summer, it may be uncomfortably *cold* this winter—unless you do something about it. All this week a consultant will be available at Kelly's Hardware to advise you and answer your questions about home insulation. And of course, Kelly's Hardware handles all the materials and tools you will need to do the work yourself. So don't let the winter winds penetrate your home in the coming months. Visit Kelly's Hardware, 1604 Main Street, in Centerville.

This spot contains 92 words. That means you would have to read at a brisk pace to make it in 30 seconds. Try it and see if it is comfortable for you.

PUBLIC SERVICE ANNOUNCEMENTS

Some spots are not commercial but public service announcements. These will be heard on both commercial and noncommercial stations. A public service announcement is one for which no fee is charged and which publicizes the cause or activities of a noncommercial organization. The principles are applied in the same way as they are for the commercial announcement. The PSA is still important even though the station is not receiving revenue for it. The copywriter should give it just as much attention, and the announcer should read it with just as much enthusiasm. The only difference is that you are selling an idea or a service rather than a product. Here is a typical 30-second public service spot announcement:

Employment Action Council

30 seconds

Kill: TFN

Last year, in Detroit, over a thousand people lined up outside an auto factory to be interviewed for a job on the assembly line. The company had one job opening. Scenes like this, repeated daily throughout the nation, tell us that there are thousands of jobless Americans who want to work. This year the week starting on Labor Day has been designated *Full Employment Week*. If you want to make America work and participate in this year's efforts, please write to Abe Vigoda, Hollywood, California. You can help make AMERICA WORK.

This Announcement has been brought to you as a public service by the Full Employment Action Council.

This spot has 91 words. The line at the end makes it over a hundred, so you would really have to hustle to get it into 30 seconds. Notice that it is necessary to give the credit at the end because the copy does not mention the Full Employment Action Council by name.

FREE–SPEECH MESSAGES

Another type of announcement that is commonly heard on radio is the free-speech message. This differs from the public service announcement in that it is the expression of an opinion on a controversial issue. It can be given by an individual or by the spokesman for a group. The message may express ideas for change or improvement in areas of community concern. It may be critical of a cause, an idea, or a concept, but it may not attack an individual's character or integrity. It must not be slanderous or obscene. The free-speech message is subject to the same restrictions that are placed upon any other broadcast communication. Stations are not required to carry free-speech messages, and some choose not to. Those that do usually say that they will accept the messages of *responsible* spokespersons. The station reserves to itself the right to determine what is to be considered responsible.

Preparing the Message

The free-speech message must first be submitted to the station in writing. It should be typed (double-spaced) and approximately 125 words in length. The statement should be mailed to the public affairs director of a station that you know carries free-speech messages. Be sure to include your name, address, and telephone number. If your message is selected, you will be invited to come to the station to record it. The message should state the identity of the speaker, the name of the group the speaker represents, and the purpose of the message. After you have said that, present the factual background, the statement of your views, and the action you want people to take. Your message might read something like this:

> My name is Tara O'Leary Hudson, and I'm asking everyone to stop buying products from countries that continue to kill whales. Hundreds of Russian and Japanese seamen are combing the Pacific Ocean right now to kill whales. Japan and Russia take about 40% of the annual catch and are the only countries engaged in deep-sea whaling. Other nations, such as Norway, Chile, and Portugal, conduct smaller-scale whaling operations from land stations.
>
> The U.S. Congress, United Nations, and others support a ten-year moratorium on whaling in order to save the whale. The International Whaling Commission, a sixteen-nation regulatory agency which includes Russia and Japan, does not agree.
>
> I feel the only way to make an impact on these countries is to stop buying their products. Write to your congressional representative and ask for limits to be placed on the imports of the countries that kill whales.

The broadcasting station will probably accept the announcement, unless there is some reason for them not to run it. If your attack is launched against a particular product that is advertised on the station, your message would probably not be aired. The FCC permits stations to decline to broadcast announcements that are contrary to their own best interests. The message that we have used as an example here might not be run by a station that advertises a considerable number of Japanese products. It is their privilege to make this choice. Free-speech messages in support of candidates running for office would also not be accepted, because airing such messages would impose the obligation to give equal time to all the other candidates.

Usually free-speech messages are concerned with local issues. They provide an excellent opportunity for the public to have access to the media.

WRITING THE NEWS COPY

Being a radio news reporter involves more than just having a good voice. You also have to be able to write news copy. Almost all news broadcasters you hear have had some basic journalism training. Your preparation for radio work should certainly include experience with print journalism as well as a consciousness of current events. You have to know the fundamentals before you can even begin to think about being a broadcast journalist. The station you work for may or may not put a heavy emphasis upon news. If they do not, they may simply require their disk jockeys to tear off a few items from the teletype and read them as a newscast every hour or so. This practice is referred to pejoratively as "rip-and-read." A much better practice is for the copy to be rewritten in the individual style of the station or of the announcer who is reporting the news. A professional newscaster will also want to include local stories that may not have been covered by the national news syndicates. In addition, there are local angles to national stories which the news reporter should investigate and develop. The information that forms the content of the story will be obtained either by firsthand experience or by talking with the people who have had some contact with the event. Once the information is gathered, it must be written up in a style that is clear, direct, and to the point.

Writing the Lead

The "lead" is the first part of a news story that gives the essential information. It tells *who* did *what, when,* and *where.* Here is an example of a lead sentence:

> President Carter held a news conference in Washington today.

In that one sentence the listener has the information needed to understand what the story is about. Later you can add the information *how* and *why.* Do not make the mistake of trying to pack too many words into the lead sentence. In broadcast you can not use the same journalistic style as that employed by the print media. The following lead might be appropriate for a newspaper story, but not for a radio broadcast:

> President Carter, in a nationally televised news conference, asked Congress on Saturday to junk the welfare system and replace it with a 34-billion-dollar plan to move able-bodied recipients into jobs and provide cash for those who can't work, but he could not say when the new system would achieve its ultimate goal of actually reducing the total amount of money the American people pay for welfare.

That lead would be understandable to a person reading it in print, but it is difficult to follow when it is being read out loud. To convert the story into a style appropriate for broadcast, a copywriter could develop the paragraph in the following way:

President Carter outlined a new welfare program today. In a nationally televised news conference he asked Congress to junk the present welfare system and replace it with a plan to move able-bodied recipients into jobs and provide cash for those who can't work. The new plan would cost about 34 billion dollars. He could not say when the new system would achieve its goal of actually reducing the total amount of money the American people pay for welfare.

Notice how much easier it is to read out loud when it is written in four sentences rather than one. There are about the same number of words, but the second writing gives you a chance to take a breath. It is not hard to get the *who, when,* and *where* into one sentence, but sometimes the *what* gets complicated. State it as simply as you can (" . . . outlined a new welfare program . . . "), and then add the details in later sentences. Try not to use more than two clauses in one sentence.

Fire broke out last night at a West Side hotel in downtown Centerville. It was the fourth in three weeks in that area and Fire Chief Alan Jones says they all appear to be the work of an arsonist.

In this lead, the *what, when,* and *where* appear in the first sentence; the *who,* with more details, is in the second sentence. You could write the lead in other ways, depending upon what you want to emphasize:

Fire Chief Alan Jones is looking for an arsonist today who may have set four fires in downtown Centerville. The latest broke out last night at a West Side hotel.

In this lead *who* and *what* are in the first sentence; *when* and *where* in the second. Later in the story you might also include *how:*

Chief Jones explained that in each of the four cases a gasoline can was found in the vicinity of the fire's origin. He said that the arsonist made little effort to conceal the fact that the fire was deliberately set.

And still later, *why:*

While there is no evidence to link the fires to a particular group, Chief Jones expressed the belief there was political motivation behind the acts. He said he thought it was more than just a coincidence that the fires began right after the county's extensive layoff of employees.

The Development

At this point you may wish to insert the voice of the fire chief giving further elaboration on his theory. But the lead would have to come first. Tell your audience the *main idea* before you load them up with details. If you do not have the actual voice of the fire chief, you may want to include more details in your own words.

Quantitative Information   Numbers and amounts are often important in a report. Remember they have to be read out loud, not perceived from the printed word. In the copy, numbers should appear the way you want them said:

$1,247 should be written "one thousand 247 dollars."

As a general rule, write the words *thousand, million,* and *billion;* also single numbers *one* through *nine;* use Arabic numerals for 10 through 999. There are exceptions to this rule, however. *Years* should be written in numerals:

A new 1980 automobile.

Round off numbers whenever you can—particularly large sums of money. If the amount is four million 537 thousand, call it

A little over four and a half million

If a number is a fraction, use the word rather than the figure.

The cost of living went up six-tenths of one percent.

When giving dates, write them out the conventional way

April 3, 1976, not 4/3/76

Add the suffix when the year is not given.

April 3rd

Keep in mind that too many numbers will get confusing, so use them sparingly. Remember that the listener is not looking over your shoulder and cannot see the copy as you can.

Quotations and Attributive Phrases   People make news. You might say that events make news, but events are important only insofar as they affect people. As mentioned in the previous chapter, most of your stories will come from people who are or were directly involved in the event. Make sure that you get the full name of the person, his or her title, and his or her relationship to the event. Is this the person who made the decision? An eyewitness? An authority on the subject? The confidence the listeners have in the source will determine whether or not they will accept the validity of the story. If the person is expressing an opinion, make sure the listener understands that. Do not let such opinions sound like your own. You can say that Chief Jones believes the fire to be the work of arsonists, without expressing that belief yourself. You are reporting the facts (what the chief *said*) rather than giving testimony of your own.

The *attributive phrase* is one which tells the source of the information. It could refer to an individual or an organization. Never use the pronoun "they" without telling who "they" are.

Poor: . . . In Washington they say that more trouble is brewing in Angola.

Better: In Washington the Defense Department indicates more trouble is brewing in Angola.

Try to avoid using the *passive voice* which tends to bypass responsibility.

Poor: . . . Development of the B-1 bomber has been considered an essential part of our national security.

Better: . . . The Pentagon has considered the development of the B-1 bomber essential to our national security.

In newspaper journalism the attributive phrase is generally put at the end of the quotation. This style is perfectly acceptable in print, but not in broadcast. Put the attributive phrase at the *beginning* of the quote; if possible make it an *indirect* rather than a *direct* quote.

Newspaper style: . . . "Three more schools will be closed in the Middletown District this fall as a result of declining enrollment caused by a decrease in the population," said School Superintendent Roger Albright in his message today to the Parent-Teachers Association.

Broadcast style: . . . School Superintendent Roger Albright said today that three more schools would be closed this fall in the Middletown District. He explained that it was the result of declining enrollment caused by a decrease in the population.

In this example the indirect quote conveys the meaning just as effectively as a direct quote and it reads much more smoothly. If the words spoken are unique and contrast in style with the language of the reporter, then the word "quote" should be written into the copy:

. . . He went on to say that to do otherwise would be, and we quote, "Fiscal irresponsibility bordering on criminal negligence." Furthermore he said that . .

Note that it is not necessary to say "Unquote." It is clear where the quotation has ended. As alternatives to the word "quote" you can use such phrases as "In his words . . ." or "As he said . . ." which mean the same thing. Remember that the listener can not hear the quotation marks that are written on the page.

Specific Details   The amount of detail you include in a news story will depend upon the policy of the station. You may not want to include as many details as you would in television or newspaper writing. Television may have newscasts running an hour or more in length. This is possible because there are film clips and visuals to hold the interest of the audience. Newspapers can print many details because people can simply stop reading when they want. But in a radio report it may be difficult to sustain interest for an extended period of time with nothing more than the auditory stimulus. This is not to say that radio stations should not attempt it. Some do successfully. But the chances of holding the attention of a large audience for more than a half hour on a single topic are slim. It may be accomplished with a variety of voices, *actualities,*[1] and *sound effects,* but it requires considerable creativity and excellent timing. An all-news station is quite expensive to operate. You must have a much larger and more highly paid staff than is required by a music station; yet you must still command a sizable audience in order to produce the necessary revenue. Most all-news stations do not expect to hold the same audience for an extended period. While they appear to be giving news in depth, they are actually repeating the highlights of important stories every hour or so. Seldom is more than one or two minutes given to a single item—usually the length is 20 to 40 seconds.

Style and Form

Writing news for radio requires a certain amount of discipline. It is not the same as free-form or creative writing. There is a procedure that must be followed for very practical reasons. It is of paramount importance that the copy be clearly understood—not just by you, but by any announcer who may be called upon to read it. When you begin doing newscasts on the air you will see the reason for the rules. They were not invented arbitrarily; they are commonsense principles that you would probably be able to figure out yourself.

Type and Double-Space   The first prerequisite for any journalist is to know how to type. Writing in longhand will just not do. Double- (or triple-) space to make the copy easy to read or correct if necessary. You may find writing in capital letters makes reading easier still.

---

[1] The term *actuality* refers to the actual voice of the newsmaker.

Include a Heading　　In the upper right-hand corner of the page write a headline, date, time, and your name. The headline can be brief, just enough to identify the story.

> City Council Meeting
> 6/14/78
> 11 PM news
> Shirley Edwards

It is important to give the date and time so that the reader will be properly oriented. The copy may have been written for the 11 P.M. news and repeated the following morning. Obviously the morning reporter would not want to say, "The action was taken at tonight's meeting."

End Each Page with a Period　　Do not carry a sentence over to another page. The reader will find it awkward to turn the page in the middle of a sentence. Better still, try to end each page with a completed paragraph.

Make Corrections Clearly　　Do not use the proofreader's correction symbols commonly employed by newspaper editors. If a word is to be deleted, block it out completely so the reader will not attempt to pronounce it. Write the correct word directly above.

> 　　　　　　　　　　　　　city
> Poor . . . The entire ~~county~~ would be affected by the ordinance.
>
> 　　　　　　　　　　　　　　city
> Better . . . The entire/~~county~~ would be affected by the ordinance.

If words must be transposed, rewrite the entire phrase.

> Poor . . . The envelope did⌐contain⌐not⌐ the correct address.
>
> 　　　　　　　　　　　did not contain
> Better . . . The envelope/~~did contain not~~ the correct address.

If too many mistakes are made in the copy, type it over. Reading the news is difficult enough under the best of circumstances; try not to impose additional hardships.

Spell Out Words Completely　　Under most circumstances, do not abbreviate. Names of states, for example, may not be easily perceived if they are abbreviated. Write Pennsylvania, not Pa.; Maine, not Me. Especially, do not abbreviate common words, such as "approx." for "approximately" and "assoc." for "association." There are some exceptions, however. You may abbreviate "Mr." and "Dr." because they are easily recognizable. But do not abbreviate less common titles:

> President Carter . . . (not Pres.)
> Captain Anderson . . . (not Capt.)
> Lieutenant Richards . . . (not Lt.)

Use Words, Not Initials If you feel that there may be doubt about the identity of an organization, refer to it by name, not by initials. You may know that NAB stands for National Association of Broadcasters, but the public may not. Spell out the words the first time you refer to the organization; after that you may use initials. Use a hyphen between the letters to separate them.

> U-A-W (United Auto Workers)
> F-A-A (Federal Aviation Administration)

Some organizations can be referred to by initials, but only when they are easily recognized.

> F-B-I
> Y-M-C-A

If the initials form an acronym, leave out the hyphen between letters so that it will be pronounced as a word.

> UNESCO
> NASA

Spell out the words United States except when it is used as an adjective.

> . . . He attempted to explain U-S foreign policy. . . . . . . The United States will receive shipments. . . .

Identify Unfamiliar People and Places It is especially important that you not start a story by using a name not well known. Instead, refer to the title or position that is familiar.

Poor: Richard Anderson was one of five people seriously injured in a freeway collision last night. He is the newest member of the County Board of Supervisors.

Better: The newest member of the County Board of Supervisors, Richard Anderson, was one of five people seriously injured in a freeway collision last night.

In the same way, make sure the listener is oriented when you refer to a place that is not generally known.

Always remember that you are in the business of communication and that communication does not take place unless other people understand what you mean. After you have finished writing a piece of copy, read it over as though you were completely unfamiliar with the story. Ask yourself if you have said it as clearly and as directly as it could be said.

SUMMARY

A great deal of copy must be written by radio station personnel every day. The person who is able to type and compose copy will be a valuable employee to the station. Most of the commercial copy is produced by advertising departments and agencies, but much of it is written by the station personnel. The student of broadcasting can obtain valuable experience in writing for radio by composing public service announcements and free-speech messages. If these are prepared in proper form they may be accepted by the radio station and put on the air. Many opportunities are available in broadcasting for the person who can write. Stations that emphasize news will often employ a large department of newswriters. Most newswriters for radio have had some journalistic background and have an interest in current events. The writer should be aware of what is going on nationally and also be able to develop the local interest angle. Local news is generally not covered by the major wire services, so virtually all of that copy needs to be generated by the station's newswriting staff. The form and style of the news story written for radio is different from that of the print media. The professional broadcast newswriter must be able to prepare copy designed to be heard rather than seen.

TERMINOLOGY

Attributive phrase	Lead
Copy	PSA
Direct quote	Rip-and-read
Free-speech message	Spot
Indirect quote	TFN
Kill date	

ACTIVITIES

1 Practice reading the spot announcements in this chapter in the time designated. Rewrite one of the announcements to make it a 1-minute spot. Rewrite the other one to make it a 10-second spot.
2 Visit some merchants who advertise on the radio. Find out how successful radio advertising has been for them. Ask who writes the copy and how often it is changed. See if they will give you some copy that you can bring to class.

3 Contact a nonprofit organization in your community. Get the necessary information, and write a public service announcement for them.

4 Select a story from the newspaper, and rewrite it in broadcast style. Read it out loud into a tape recorder. Give the copy to a friend or fellow student in your broadcast class, and see if it can be read easily by another person. Repeat the exercise until you can rewrite a news story quickly, easily, and clearly. Save the copy that you write, and put it together in the form of a complete newscast.

5 Write a firsthand news story. Select an event that you can cover personally. Attend a news conference, lecture, courtroom hearing, or legislative session. Take notes as you listen; be sure to get the full names of the people to whom you will want to refer. Sift through your notes and select the most important information. Write your news story; then record it and see how it sounds.

6 If you are working for a college or community station, phone in a news story and have it recorded through a phone patch. You can either read from copy you have written or ad lib it. Your voice can then be used as an actuality in a newscast.

Chapter 12

Gathering and Reporting the News

RADIO AS A NEWS MEDIUM

The important advantage radio has over other media is immediacy. Fast-breaking news items can be transmitted to millions of people with a minimum of effort. There was a time when newspapers competed fiercely to be the first on the streets with a news story. Newsboys would cry out, "Extra! Extra!" and sometimes recite the headline. But this colorful scene is no longer a part of the American Parade. By the time a newspaper gets on the streets, most people have already heard the story on radio or have seen it on television. Why then do people read newspapers at all? The answer to that question is complex, but there are a few fundamental reasons. First, print is still the best device for conveying stories in depth. You can read to yourself much faster than someone else can read to you. There are not enough words in a 30-minute radio news program to fill the front page of a major newspaper. Try it sometime. See how long it takes you to read aloud (in radio announcer's style) the entire front page of a newspaper. Another advantage of print is that it provides a permanent record of events. With the aid of an index, you can go directly to the section of the paper you want—sports, stock market reports, entertainment, etc. If you relied upon radio, you would have to wait for a particular item to be aired, and you might not know when it would be coming—if at all. When it did come you would have to write it down to have a record of it. It is clear that print journalism and broadcast journalism differ in both style and purpose.

WHAT IS NEWS?

Journalists could spend hours debating this question; let us provide a brief definition. We shall say that news is current information presented without malice or favoritism. It should be reported as objectively as possible. David Brinkley has said that, while it may be impossible to be objective in news reporting, one can at least be *fair*. This is about all you can do. Obviously all the news can not be made available to people— there is not enough time or space. Therefore, reporters *select* the items they think are important. In doing so they are making editorial judgments. If they desired, they could effectively persuade the population to accept a point of view, not by telling any lies, but simply by omitting news items that suggested an opposing point of view. In this country, freedom of the press is more than just political jargon: It is an actuality. The restrictions government places upon broadcasters are those that assure fair treatment for everyone. For example, you are not free to make untrue or slanderous statements about an individual. You are also not free to use a public commodity (the airwaves) to support one political candidate over another. You are free, however, to report on events, even though they be embarrassing to those in power. No government restriction prevented the exposure of the Watergate scandal. Your main concern as a broadcast journalist is not the limitation placed upon you by government, but those imposed by the audience. You are free to say pretty much what you want, but your message will not be heard unless you gain and hold the attention of the listeners.

SELECTING NEWS ITEMS

Out of the myriad of events that occur every day, what items are you going to select? The broad, general areas will be determined by the programming department and will depend upon the particular audience segment the station wishes to reach. If the station is playing "middle of the road" (MOR) music and is appealing to a mature, educated audience between 35 and 50 years of age and enjoying some economic affluence, you will probably offer stock market reports and financial news. If you are playing *contemporary rock* music for a younger audience, your news features would probably include sports and entertainment. The *progressive rock* stations would offer features such as drug reports and news about the latest occult fad. But the choices are unlimited. *Anything that can be put into words can be put on the radio.*

WIRE SERVICES

Most stations subscribe to at least one news wire service. There are three major ones in the English language: The Associated Press (AP), United Press International (UPI), and Reuters (a British firm). They feed news onto teletype machines located in subscribing stations by way of a telephone wire—thus the name "wire service." The teletype runs 24 hours a day and brings in news from all parts of the world. The subscriber has access to the stories and features of hundreds of reporters—a service no broadcaster could possibly finance alone. The advantage of the wire service is that it allows broad coverage and makes available information that a station would otherwise not be able to obtain. The disadvantage is that it puts the job of selecting news items into the hands of relatively few people. Figure 12-1 shows some UPI teletype machines.

Figure 12-1   Teletype machines. *(Courtesy UPI.)*

Just about all the news we receive from abroad is filtered through the news services. We rarely hear what they think is unimportant. For this reason, local stations should not rely totally on news services. It is very easy for announcers simply to "rip and read." That means accepting blindly the judgment of the wire service and reading what they send out as a news summary. The discriminating newsperson will use the wire service as a foundation, but add to it her or his own stories and local angles on national events. Figure 12-2 shows a typical news summary as it would be received by a station from one of the major wire services.

Figure 12-2 World news summary. *(Courtesy UPI.)*

```
215LR
    THIRD-WORLD NEWS ROUNDUP
    -6-
    PRESIDENT CARTER'S IMPENDING TRIP TO THE MIDDLE EAST... A NEW
MIDEAST CRISIS LOOMING-- THIS TIME INVOLVING NORTH AND SOUTH YEMEN...
AN UPDATE ON THE FIGHTING IN INDOCHINA... AND NEWS ABOUT ENERGY...
    ALL PART OF TONIGHT'S ROUNDUP-- SIGNIFICANT NEWS... REPORTED IN
DETAIL... BY U-P-I:
    -6-
    (MIDEAST)
    THE GENERAL SHAPE OF PRESIDENT CARTER'S MIDEAST PEACE PACKAGE
EMERGED TODAY WITH DISCLOSURE OF AN ASSORTMENT OF AMERICAN PROPOSALS
AIMED AT REACHING AN EGYPTIAN-ISRAELI TREATY.
    THE HEART OF THE PACKAGE THAT CARTER WILL TAKE WITH HIM TO THE
MIDDLE EAST THIS WEEK IS A PROPOSAL FOR EGYPT AND ISRAEL TO TRADE OFF
THE TWO KEY ISSUES IN DISPUTE.
    ISRAEL WOULD GO ALONG WITH EGYPT'S INSISTENCE ON A TIMETABLE FOR
SOME FORM OF PALESTINIAN SELF-RULE IN OCCUPIED TERRITORIES... WHILE
EGYPT WOULD ACCEPT ISRAEL'S DEMAND THAT THE TREATY SUPERSEDE ALL
OTHERS WITH EGYPT'S ARAB ALLIES.
    THE ISRAELI CABINET HAS ALREADY ACCEPTED THE TRADE-OFF IN
PRINCIPAL. TWO OF CARTER'S TOP ADVISERS SOUNDED EGYPT OUT ON THE
PROPOSAL TODAY... WITH INITIAL INDICATIONS APPEARING FAVORABLE.
    CARTER'S PEACE PACKAGE ALSO INCLUDES PROPOSALS TO PROVIDE ISRAEL
WITH OIL AND MILITARY AID.
    (YEMEN)
    IT'S ONLY A LITTLE WAR... BUT A BIG THREAT TO POLITICAL STABILITY
AT THE SOUTHERN OUTLET OF THE OIL-RICH RED SEA REGION.
    TEN DAYS OF FIGHTING AND BROKEN CEASE-FIRE AGREEMENTS BETWEEN TINY
```

NORTH YEMEN AND EQUALLY TINY SOUTH YEMEN ARE CAUSING DEEP CONCERN IN NEIGHBORING SAUDI ARABIA.

THE UNITED STATES SHOWED ITS CONCERN TODAY BY ORDERING THE SUPERCARRIER CONSTELLATION TO SAIL FROM ITS BASE IN THE PHILIPPINES TO THE ARABIAN SEA.

PENTAGON SOURCES SAY THE CONSTELLATION'S ORDERS WERE CUT AFTER SECRETARY OF STATE CYRUS VANCE REJECTED MOSCOW'S CLAIMS THAT THE SOVIETS ARE NOT HELPING THE MARXIST REGIME IN SOUTH YEMEN.

BOTH WARRING COUNTRIES TODAY ACCUSED EACH OTHER OF STARTING FRESH BATTLES ALONG THEIR ILL-DEFINED BORDER.

(ENERGY)

ENERGY SECRETARY JAMES SCHLESINGER TOLD CONGRESS TODAY THAT THE FUEL CRUNCH IS BECOMING SO CRITICAL THAT AMERICAN MOTORISTS FACE GASOLINE SHORTAGES OVER THE NEXT TWO SUMMERS.

SCHLESINGER'S TESTIMONY BEFORE A HOUSE SUBCOMMITTEE UNDERSCORED HIS EARLIER PREDICTION THAT GASOLINE PRICES COULD RISE TO ONE DOLLAR A GALLON FOR UNLEADED AND 75 CENTS FOR LEADED GRADES BY THE END OF THE YEAR.

THERE WAS ALSO MORE DISCOURAGING NEWS FROM FOREIGN OIL FIELDS.

LIBYA RAISED PRICES BY ONE-DOLLAR 30-CENTS A BARREL... AND ALGERIA SAID IT'S PLANNING A 24 PERCENT HIKE.

AIR TRAVELERS ARE ALSO FEELING THE PINCH.

SHORTAGE OF JET FUEL IN CHICAGO TODAY FORCED DELTA AIR LINES TO CANCEL 18 FLIGHTS SCHEDULED TO ARRIVE OR DEPART FROM O'HARE INTERNATIONAL AIRPORT.

UNITED AIRLINES ALSO HAS BEGUN ELIMINATING UP TO 39 DAILY FLIGHTS FROM CHICAGO AND EASTERN CITIES.

(CENSUS)

THE CENSUS BUREAU RELEASED A STUDY TODAY SHOWING THE DROPOUT RATE AMONG BLACK HIGH SCHOOL STUDENTS HAS FALLEN SUBSTANTIALLY IN RECENT YEARS.

THE REPORT ALSO SAYS THE NUMBER OF BLACKS ATTENDING COLLEGE MORE THAN DOUBLED DURING THE 1970S.

AND THE BUREAU NOTES THAT BLACK STUDENTS WHO ENROLL IN HIGH SCHOOL OR COLLEGE ARE NOW LESS LIKELY TO DROP BEHIND IN THEIR STUDIES.

CURRENT ENROLLMENT RATES SUGGEST THAT THE DIFFERENCE BETWEEN BLACK AND WHITE HIGH SCHOOL GRADUATION LEVELS WILL DECREASE EVEN FURTHER IN THE NEXT 10 YEARS.

THE CENSUS REPORT GOES ON TO SAY THERE IS EVIDENCE THAT AMONG

```
THOSE GRADUATING HIGH SCHOOL... BLACKS AND WHITES ARE ATTENDING
COLLEGE AT ABOUT THE SAME RATE-- 32 PERCENT.

   (NUCLEAR)

OFFICIALS OF AMERICAN NUCLEAR INSURERS-- A GROUP THAT INSURES
ATOMIC POWER PLANTS-- HAVE RELEASED A STATEMENT SAYING THOSE ATOMIC
PLANTS HAVE ONE OF THE NATION'S BEST INDUSTRIAL SAFETY RECORDS.

   BUT THE INSURANCE GROUP SAYS ITS STANDARDS MAY HAVE TO BE REVISED
SOON BECAUSE OF NEW CONCERN ABOUT RADIATION RISKS.

   THE OFFICIALS SAY THAT... IN RECENT YEARS... THERE'S BEEN AN
INCREASE IN THE NUMBER OF WORKERS CLAIMING THAT RADIATION EXPOSURE
HAS DAMAGED THEIR HEALTH.

   THEY CITE PUBLICITY SURROUNDING A NEW REPORT BY THE HEALTH,
EDUCATION AND WELFARE DEPARTMENT AS ONE OF THE REASONS FOR THE
INCREASE.

   THE H-E-W REPORT CONCERNS THE NEGATIVE EFFECTS OF LOW-LEVEL
RADIATION ON HEALTH.
          UPI 03-06 06:08 PPS
```

The wire service may also provide the radio station with short, spot summaries, or headlines, to be used in between the longer newscasts.

Figure 12-3   World news headlines. *(Courtesy UPI.)*

```
263LR
   HEADLINES
   -0-
   PRESIDENT CARTER LEAVES FOR EGYPT WEDNESDAY FOR TALKS WITH
PRESIDENT SADAT ABOUT U-S PROPOSALS FOR BREAKING THE DEADLOCK IN
EGYPT'S STALLED PEACE NEGOTIATIONS WITH ISRAEL. TWO TOP CARTER AIDES
HAVE ALREADY SHOWN THOSE PROPOSALS TO SADAT.


   ISRAELI PRIME MINISTER BEGIN WAS QUOTED AS TELLING JEWISH LEADERS
IN NEW YORK THE QUESTION OF SETTING A DATE FOR PALESTINIAN AUTONOMY
IN OCCUPIED ARAB LANDS HAS BEEN, QUOTING HERE-- "TAKEN CARE OF."
   -0-
   DEFENSE SOURCES IN WASHINGTON SAY A SOVIET COMBAT SHIP HAS GONE
INTO PORT IN THE VIETNAMESE CITY OF DANANG. THE SOVIET VESSEL IS AN
AMPHIBIOUS VEHICLE THAT CAN CARRY TANKS, TRUCKS AND TROOPS.
          UPI 03-06 09:09 FPS
```

Figure 12-4 Sports and weather. *(Courtesy UPI.)*

FIRST-SPORTS ROUNDUP

-4-

(BASEBALL)

MAJOR LEAGUE BASEBALL BEGINS ITS 1979 CAMPAIGN TODAY. THE
TRADITIONAL NATIONAL LEAGUE OPENER WILL BE PLAYED THIS AFTERNOON
(2:30 P-M E-S-T) AT RIVERFRONT STADIUM, WHERE THE CINCINNATI REDS
HOST THE SAN FRANCISCO GIANTS. VIDA BLUE... AN 18-GAME WINNER FOR THE
GIANTS LAST YEAR... WILL OPPOSE TOM SEAVER, WHO IS COMING OFF A
SUB-PAR 16-14 SEASON.

THE REDS BEGIN THE SEASON WITHOUT PETE ROSE... WHO SIGNED WITH
PHILADELPHIA DURING THE OFF-SEASON... AND SPARKY ANDERSON, WHO WAS
FIRED AS MANAGER. JOHN MCNAMARA... THE REDS' NEW SKIPPER... HAS
PENCILED SPEEDSTER KEN GRIFFEY IN THE LEADOFF SPOT AND RAY KNIGHT IS
SLATED TO TAKE ROSE'S PLACE AT THIRD BASE.

SEVEN-TIME AMERICAN LEAGUE BATTING CHAMPION ROD CAREW MAKES HIS
OFFICIAL DEBUT FOR CALIFORNIA TONIGHT WHEN THE ANGELS TRAVEL TO
SEATTLE FOR THE AMERICAN LEAGUE OPENER. CAREW LED THE CACTUS LEAGUE
WITH 18 RUNS-BATTED-IN THIS SPRING AND, BECAUSE OF HIS BAT, THE
ANGELS ARE FAVORED IN THE AMERICAN LEAGUE WEST. CALIFORNIA WILL SEND
SOUTHPAW FRANK TANANA (TAH-NAN'-AH) TO THE MOUND AGAINST THE
MARINERS' GLENN ABBOTT.

-4-

(UMPS)

ONLY TWO MAJOR LEAGUE UMPIRES HAVE SIGNED CONTRACTS FOR THE '79
SEASON, FORCING THE PROMOTION OF MINOR LEAGUE UMPIRES FOR OPENING DAY
ASSIGNMENTS. GLENN ABBOTT... SEATTLE'S OPENING DAY PITCHER... SAYS HE
DOESN'T ANTICIPATE ANY PROBLEM WORKING WITH INEXPERIENCED UMPIRES. HE
SAYS THEY WERE VERY CONSISTENT IN SPRING TRAINING.

-4-

(PHILLIES)

THE PHILADELPHIA PHILLIES HAVE TRADED ROOKIE SHORTSTOP TODD CRUZ
TO THE KANSAS CITY ROYALS IN AN ATTEMPT TO SHORE UP THEIR
INJURY-RIDDLED PITCHING STAFF. IN RETURN FOR CRUZ, THE PHILLIES
RECEIVED DOUG BIRD, WHO HAD AN 11-4 RECORD AND 14 SAVES WITH THE
ROYALS IN 1977. HOWEVER, BIRD'S RECORD SLIPPED TO 6-6 LAST SEASON
WITH ONLY ONE SAVE. CRUZ BATTED .261 AT OKLAHOMA CITY LAST SEASON
WITH 11 HOME RUNS AND 69 R-B-I'S.

-4-

```
    (A'S)

    CHARLIE FINLEY'S LATEST ATTEMPT TO SELL THE OAKLAND A'S TO A GROUP
    OF CALIFORNIA BUSINESSMEN APPARENTLY HAS FALLEN THROUGH. FINLEY
    REPORTEDLY IS UNHAPPY WITH THE FINANCIAL ARRANGEMENTS.
       -4-
    (EASTER)
    FUNERAL SERVICES WERE HELD IN CLEVELAND YESTERDAY FOR FORMER
    INDIANS' FIRST BASEMAN LUKE EASTER. FORMER TEAMMATES IN ATTENDANCE
    INCLUDED NEW YORK YANKEES' MANAGER BOB LEMON, YANKEE PRESIDENT AL
    ROSEN, HALL OF FAME PITCHER BOB FELLER AND PITCHER MIKE GARCIA.
    EASTER WAS SHOT AND KILLED LAST THURSDAY DURING A ROBBERY IN A
    CLEVELAND SUBURB.
       UPI 04-03 11:07 PPS

237LR
    EXTENDED-FORECASTS FRIDAY THROUGH SUNDAY
       -3-
    NORTHERN CALIFORNIA-- MOSTLY FAIR AND DRY BUT CHANCE OF SHOWERS
    FRIDAY MAINLY IN MOUNTAINS AND VARIABLE LOW CLOUDS ON COAST. HIGHS IN
    THE MID 50S TO MID 60S NEAR THE COAST AND THE MID 60S TO MID 70S
    INLAND VALLEYS. LOWS IN THE 40S TO LOW 50S AT LOW ELEVATIONS.
```

You will notice that between the stories there is a numeral or a character to separate each item from the next—UPI uses -0- or sometimes numbers as spacers. These are cues provided for the reader of the copy to drop the voice. The news services accommodate broadcasting stations by sending out a 5-minute summary every hour. Because radio stations often program news on the hour, the summary is timed to be received before the top of every hour. However, it may not be sent all at the same time. Other news, such as baseball scores and weather reports, may come in between the items of a 5-minute summary. So you will have to study the copy well to make sure you get everything you want. You do not have to take it the way the wire service sends it. You can take any part of it you want and arrange it in any order. If you are involved in selecting news from the teletype machine, there are a few things you need to do:

1 *Get the latest copy.* The copy is received by the station on one long, continuous roll. Unless it gets thrown out at the end of the day, you may wind up reading yesterday's or last week's copy without realizing it. Look for the date that appears at the bottom of each story. Then look for the number at the top of each story. The highest number will be the latest release.

2 *Proofread the copy.* The people who type out the stories are working under a great deal of pressure. It is not uncommon for them to make mistakes in typing. Sometimes the machine itself will cause the copy to be garbled. This can be very embarrassing when you are reading the story on the air "cold."

3 *Note corrections in the copy.* Wire services may print information that is incorrect or needs to be updated. When this happens, they will type out a correction message that refers to a story by number. It may say something like this:

```
                 C O R R E C T I O N

      IN SIXTH SUMMARY, TAKE 3, FIRST ITEM (SEOUL), READ IT IN FIRST
SENTENCE OF SECOND GRAF:  X X X TO REVIEW THE INCIDENT SATURDAY (10
P.M. EDT FRIDAY) X X X (FIXING TYPO).


   THE A-P
```

4 *Look for special features.* Not all the copy that comes in on the teletype is straight news. Much of it is feature material—sometimes humorous, sometimes human interest. It may come in a regular feature, or it may be mixed in with the other items. Usually human interest features are placed at the end of the newscast.

5 *Look and listen for bulletins.* When an important, late-breaking item comes in, it will be flashed as a bulletin. Simultaneously, a bell will ring on the machine to attract your attention. Use your judgment as to whether you want to interrupt the program then on the air to announce the bulletin or wait until the next regularly scheduled newscast.

Other Sources of News

Some stations prefer to write their own news rather than rely on the wire services. It is important to remember that when you take material from newspapers and magazines it must be rewritten; otherwise you could be guilty of plagiarism. When you subscribe to a wire service you are buying the rights to use what they send you, word for word. This is not the case when you subscribe to a newspaper. You can not legally duplicate the material without the publisher's permission. In addition to the legal consideration, it is necessary to rewrite newspaper copy because, as we discussed earlier, the style is substantially different. Try reading a newspaper story out loud in a radio announcer's style and see how difficult it is. This is why a station that emphasizes news needs to employ copywriters.

Stringers   In addition to the full-time staff, the news station may employ part-time reporters called *stringers.* This practice originated in the newspaper business as a means of extending coverage at minimum cost. A stringer is paid not a regular salary, but fees, according to the number of stories contributed. A stringer, happening upon a story, simply calls it in, and it is written up by a staff writer. A stringer might go directly on the air with a report, or perhaps have the story tape-recorded. The advantage to this system is that the station gets extensive coverage without having to employ a large staff. The station knows the person who is making the report and is able to count on the information's being accurate. Many news reporters have begun their careers as stringers.

Audio Feeds   In addition to the sources already mentioned, several news organizations provide *audio feeds* to subscribing stations. An audio feed is an interview or a news report that can be tape-recorded and inserted into the local program in any manner the station wishes. It is fed to the station by telephone line in the same way as the network programs are. The two major U.S. wire services, The Associated Press and United Press International, provide audio feeds in addition to their regular transmission of printed copy via teletype. There are also a number of small radio networks that provide audio feeds and regularly scheduled programs to local stations. ABC has two subsidiaries that offer such service. One is the American Contemporary Radio Network, and the other is the American FM Radio Network. They operate independently of the regular ABC news service and are available to any station that wishes to subscribe.

Other Telephone Feeds   Every local area has institutions that provide features of various sorts that are available over the telephone. Colleges and universities often have news and information agencies. Churches occasionally offer similar services. Institutions such as historical societies, medical associations, and special-interest groups frequently make information available to telephone callers. A radio station can call the number, record the message, and use it as an insert in a newscast or special feature.

Tape Networks   Some of the smaller networks provide programs to stations by means of tape recordings. Rather than incur the expense of a direct line or the cost of the telephone, the network sends the program to the station in the form of a disk transcription or tape recording. If the network is sponsored by a nonprofit organization, as many of them are, the only cost to the station would be postage. Programs in this form are available from the Broadcasting Foundation of America, the Longhorn Radio Network, and The Fund for Peace, to mention just a few.

Printed Copy   The three major wire services, AP, UPI, and Reuters, provide printed copy rapidly and abundantly to subscribing stations. Most commercial stations rely upon one or more of these services for the bulk of their locally produced newscasts. There are, however, less expensive news services that deliver copy to subscribing stations by mail rather than by teletype. The mail services are slower and can not compete with the wire services in handling fast-breaking news. But they can provide valuable background information and feature news that may not have been covered by the major sources. Mail news services such as Earth News and Zodiac News Service describe themselves as being alternative sources of current information. They are valuable to the low-budget broadcaster, but these services are often utilized by the larger stations as well.

Reliability of Information

How do you tell if the source of your information is reliable? Some sources you can trust; others may be questionable. Most major newspapers and national magazines have a reputation to maintain; they would not jeopardize that by deliberately falsifying a news story. But if you have any doubt about the source, there are a number of questions you should ask yourself:

1 Has other information from the source been accurate? What reputation does it have for providing reliable information? Has its integrity been challenged on previous occasions? If so, by whom?

2 Does the source have any obvious bias? Does it have anything to gain by reporting something in a particular way? Is there a tendency on the part of the source to look at all issues from a particular point of view? Is its management willing to print opposing viewpoints?

3 Is the information complete? Has the original source been named, or simply referred to in a vague manner? ("*They* say that . . .") Are quotations taken out of context? Does the quotation express what the person really meant?

4 Is the information current? Has new information superseded the report? Is it possible that the passage of time has altered the situation? Have new laws been passed or new statistics gathered since the story was written?

5 Do other sources corroborate the information? If so, are the *other* sources reliable? Are there reasons why one source would have the information and others not have it? Are there reasons why other sources would not want to release the information?

6 Does the information meet the test of reason? Are there internal contradictions in the information? Does the information contradict something else you know to be true?

7 Was the information gathered accurately? If it is statistical information, was there adequate sampling? Are general assertions made as though they were statements of fact? ("90 percent of the people you ask will tell you that . . .") Is the study consistent with the findings of other studies?

8 Is the language of the information objective? Is the copy spotted with emotionally "loaded" words such as "demagogue" and "tyrant"? Would more objective words convey the same meaning? Are there an excessive number of adjectives? ("An angry, vicious, uncontrollable mob . . .")

The way these questions are answered will, of course, reflect your own personal feelings and biases, but at least it will start you thinking about objective and subjective reporting.

Sources of Local News

In addition to the newspapers and magazines, the most important sources of news are the people in your community. Not everybody makes news every day; you must find the ones who have. Some are in a better position than others to provide you with news stories, and these are the ones you want to contact. Make a list of all the people and offices you can think of that could be a source of news. Be sure to include the addresses and telephone numbers. Here is a list you might use as a starter:

Agricultural Commissioner
Animal Control Department
City Council
County Board of Supervisors
County Clerk
County Tax Assessor
District Attorney
District Court
Department of Motor Vehicles
Drug Abuse Coordinator
Employment Office
Fire Department
Health Department
Hospitals

Jury Commissioner
Mayor's Office
Mental Health Clinic
Municipal Court
Office of Consumer Affairs
Office of Social Welfare
Police Department
Post Office
Public Utility Commission
School District Office
Sheriff's Office
Superior Court
Transportation Agency
Veterans' Office
Water Commission

Obtaining Actualities

You can make your contacts either by phone or in person. There are several advantages in doing it by phone: You save time and gasoline. Also, your respondent may become nervous at the sight of a microphone. Taping a reply off the telephone is much easier. People are used to that instrument and are not threatened by it. They may talk more freely when the recording equipment is not in the same room with them. However, you must be sure to tell all respondents that they are being recorded, and that you would like to use their remarks on the radio. You need not use the "beeper phone," which once was required, as long as the parties know they are being recorded. Simple phone taps are very inexpensive and easily obtained. Any electronics store will have them. (See Figure 12-5.) Get the kind with the plastic cuff that fits over the earpiece of the phone; then put the plug into the microphone input jack of your tape recorder and set your levels. The phone tap works exactly the same as a microphone. The quality will be the same as it is on the telephone. While it is not as good as it would be using a microphone, this is no real disadvantage. People are accustomed to hearing reports through a telephone and accept them readily. In fact, there is a certain authenticity to the sound of a news story coming through the filter of a phone.

These types of reports are called *actualities*. Rather than have the news reader repeat what the news maker has said, we hear the news maker's actual voice. This enhances credibility and provides variety to the sound of the report. In bypassing the intermediate steps of rewriting the material and delivering it on the air, the use of actualities saves the

Figure 12-5 Phone tap. *(Photo by Wayne Fogle.)*

news announcer considerable time and effort—and eliminates the risk of misquoting. As an example, suppose that there has been a fatal airplane accident and, as is customary, an investigation is under way. You wish to question a certain government official and include some of her answers in your coverage. Follow this simple procedure:

1 Decide on the story you want and the source that is best able to provide you with the information. Refer to the list given earlier in this chapter.

2 Connect the phone tap to your tape recorder and call the official. You will have to get through switchboard operators, secretaries, and perhaps a few junior assistant managers. But be patient, and always be courteous.

3 Start your tape recorder as soon as you get the person you want. Tell him that you are recording and would like to use his remarks on the radio. He may be willing to respond right away, or he may ask you to call back when he has had a chance to think over your questions.

4 Ask your questions. Giver him plenty of time to answer—you are going to edit out the pauses anyway. Ask as many questions as he has time to answer; you may have a hard time getting hold of him again. Remember that *your* words are being recorded too, so don't talk while he is talking. You will not be able to edit out the subverbal sounds (uh huh, hmmm) that people often make unconsciously.

5 After the interview play back the tape and decide on what statements you want to use. Dub them off onto a cart as described in Chapter 5.

6 Write the introductory material that will precede the actuality. It has to include the name and title of the person you talked to and an orienting statement about the subject. This is called a lead-in and will look something like this:

> Last night two planes collided in flight over the eastern hills of Durham county. Two people were killed; another is in serious condition. Here is a report from Roberta Darbey, local director of the Federal Aviation Administration.

Before you start working with actualities, listen to an all-news station and get some ideas on how it is done. You will notice that the actuality is generally not very long. While the reporter may have taped 20 or 30 minutes of the news maker when gathering information, the report will probably contain only a few 1- or 2-minute segments. Encapsulate your report into a form that can be digested easily by the listener. Highlight the main aspects of the story by preceding it with your own paraphrase. In other words, give a short preface to what the news maker is going to say. When you do this, use the third person pronoun rather than the second person:

> Poor: . . .Can you tell me if there was any indication that the planes were not in proper mechanical condition?
> Better: . . .We asked Ms. Darbey if there was any indication that the planes were not in proper mechanical condition.

The listener will be able to tell that you are not doing a live interview, so do not try to pretend that the news maker is there in the studio with you.

As you work with actualities you will begin to develop some refinements. For example, it is interesting to hear comments from two different people on the same subject. More interesting still when the comments in juxtaposition use the same key words, or when they express conflicting viewpoints.

> *Mayor:* I believe it is my responsibility to appoint the best people I can find to important positions in this city. If one of these people happens to be a relative of mine, it is entirely coincidental.
> *Council member:* There is nothing at all coincidental about the mayor's appointment of his cousin. A dozen other people equally qualified applied for the job months ago.

In a case such as this there is no need for a comment in between—and certainly no need for an evaluation on the part of the reporter. Let the listeners make up their own minds and draw their own conclusions. Remember, you are a news *reporter,* not a commentator. Keep your opinions to yourself. Just tell listeners what happened as clearly and as objectively as you can.

INTERVIEWING THE NEWSMAKER

Not very often will you be able to report on a news event firsthand. You may just happen to be on the scene at the time of an accident, or you may be sent by your station to get a firsthand report of a major occurrence. But most of the time you will be relying upon a description of the event given to you by someone who was directly or indirectly involved. Extracting the information from that person may not be easy because not everyone is trained in journalism or has the ability to tell a story clearly and succinctly. You will have to help them. It is your job to ask the questions that will bring forth the information you want. If you fail to ask the question, you may never get the answer; if you ask the wrong question, you may get a story you have no use for; if you ask too many questions, you will wind up with more information than you know what

Figure 12-6 Conducting an interview. *(Photo by Wayne Fogle.)*

to do with. So interviewing is a skill to which you want to give a lot of attention.

Types of Interviews

There are many types of interviews, some of which are not appropriate for broadcast. You need to apply the style that will demonstrate that you are a competent professional.

1   *Personal interview.* This is a situation where the interviewer is trying to get information for some private purpose. A job interview would fall into this category. An employer may interview an applicant to learn something about the person's qualifications for a particular job. The information is only valuable to the interviewer, not to the general public.

2   *Psychotherapeutic interview.* This is the kind conducted by a trained psychologist who attempts to draw out feelings and inner thoughts that the interviewee may not have known were there. Respondents in this type of interview may be saying things they had never expressed before. It would be unfair to put this type of interview on the air. People have the right to contemplate their feelings and ideas before making them public.

3   *Public interview.* This is the kind that concerns us in broadcasting. It is the interview that is designed to reveal information of general public interest. Although the interviewer may already know the answers to the questions asked, asking them elicits answers in the respondents' own words. A good interviewer will try to facilitate the telling of the story. This requires, of course, understanding the story, in order to know what questions to ask and to paraphrase, if necessary, a point that might not have been clearly made.

Under the heading of *public interview* there can be two divisions: hostile and friendly. I advise my students in broadcasting not to attempt a hostile interview. Sometimes you hear it done by professionals, but it takes considerable skill and experience. People such as William Buckley and Mike Wallace can do it well, but for the inexperienced broadcaster, the results can be disastrous. A hostile interview is one in which the interviewer attacks the points expressed by the respondent. Such interviews can only be done effectively by interviewers who are themselves prominent figures, whose opinions and comments are just as valid and as worthy of public consideration as those of the interviewee. The neophyte runs the danger of being outclassed by a person who is very knowledgeable in the subject. It can be embarrassing to get nailed to the wall on your own show. Even if you win the argument, listeners may object to your methods if you are abusive of your guest. So conduct a *friendly* interview even if you disagree with your respondent's point of view. Later you can interview someone else if you want to, in order to have the arguments refuted. Most people have an affinity for "fair play." In private practice we may abuse this concept, but in public we like to see it observed. A basic principle for all broadcasters is to have respect for all reasonable arguments, even when you strongly oppose them.

Conducting the Interview

In some cases an interview will be done live; at other times, you may tape it with the intention of editing it and extracting portions you want to use. Let's talk about the *live interview.*

Most important of all is to *listen to what is said.* It is very easy to become distracted. You may be thinking of the next question you are going to ask and miss the response the person is making to your previous question. In all phases of your life listening is important, but in broadcasting you risk serious embarrassment by not paying attention. A friend of mine at a small station was doing an afternoon series of live telephone interviews of women at home. He had stock questions that he always asked and seldom listened to the reply. The interview I heard went something like this:

Announcer: Tell me, Mrs. Jones, what does your husband do for a living?
Woman: Well, my husband died three months ago.
Announcer: Well, that's just wonderful Mrs. Jones, now would you tell me
. . .

Admonitions are more easily made than acted upon, but here are some suggestions that may be helpful.

1 *Start listening from the beginning.* Portions of messages are often lost when the listener fails to hear an antecedent. Speakers are not always careful about using nouns in their sentences. They may use the name of the person, place, or thing in the beginning, but after that it will be referred to by a pronoun he, she, it, they, or them. If you did not catch the noun at the start, and are failing to comprehend the message, interrupt the speaker and ask, even if this reveals that you were not listening in the beginning.

2 *Suspend judgment.* Establish, if you can, a frame of mind which allows you to listen objectively. If you begin listening with the intention of taking issue with what the speaker says or with the attitude that you are not going to agree under any circumstances, you will hear only the points of contention and miss what may be valid information. Good listening depends upon your ability to cut through your own emotional barriers and your preconceived notions about the message of the speaker. It is simply a matter of listening with an open mind. If the speaker happens to be someone you dislike, try to separate the personality from the message.

3 *Listen for the main idea.* Most people are not well trained in speaking and may not be skillful in putting forward the main idea of their message. Sometimes the example they are relating becomes more important than the point that is being illustrated. Try to perceive the main idea, but if you cannot, ask what it is. In any case, when the speaker finishes, you should be able to summarize the gist of the message.

4 *Listen for new ideas.* It is easy to listen when a speaker is relating something which you already know. What is more difficult is to listen, comprehend, and remember ideas that you are hearing for the first time. But after all, this is the only thing that is really valuable to you. Information can be most valuable when it is new or when it is phrased in a way that you have never heard before.

5 *Listen for details.* The most difficult kind of listening is that which involves information. The specifics of the message—names, dates, places, facts, figures—are much harder to assimilate than overall concepts. A good speaker will be able to give proper emphasis to the important details. But you can't always count on the speaker's being good. You may have to determine for yourself what these important specific details are. A danger involved here is that while you are mentally filing the detailed information you will miss a portion of the message that follows. A good listener is able to hold onto an overall concept and still pick up additional specific information.[1]

Advance Preparation Before you begin an interview, know something about the person and the subject. This may require going to the library or finding some source material in magazines. If there is no time for this, talk to the person beforehand and get what background information you can. Do not put yourself in the position of having to ask questions on the air that you should have asked before. When you hear an interviewer say, "How do you pronounce your last name?" or "What is your exact title?" you know that some homework has been skimped. When you go on the air you should already know these things so you can

---

[1] John Hasling, *Group Discussion and Decision Making* (New York: Thomas Y. Crowell, 1975), pp. 57–59.

get as quickly as possible to the subject matter of the interview. Remember that advance preparation is necessary so you can compact a maximum amount of material into a short space of time. Ask what questions the respondent would like to field. Be as accommodating as you can. Your guest is the one who knows the material and is the best judge of its value. You will have to select what you have time for and what will best meet the needs of your particular audience. You may not want to write out a long list of questions because that might jeopardize the spontaneity of the interview, but have at least the first few questions planned. That way you will both feel more confident, and the interview will get off to a faster start. Beginnings and endings are the most difficult.

Starting the Interview   You cannot start an interview by asking the first question; you have to orient the listener with a certain amount of information. State the preliminaries as briskly as you can; they would include the following:

1   Your name
2   The name and title of the respondent
3   The subject of the interview
4   The reason for the interview

A typical interview might begin something like this: "Good afternoon. I'm Bill White and we are talking today with Dr. Barbara Pellman who is professor emeritus at Upstate College in the field of nuclear physics. We have asked Dr. Pellman if she would comment upon the recent proposal to construct a nuclear power plant in our county. Dr. Pellman, How safe is nuclear power?"

This is pretty much a standard opening. There are variations, but they should contain the essential information. Notice that the first question gives Dr. Pellman a chance to express her overall view before going into detail. We can get a pretty good idea of where she stands by her response to it. Do not start with a question that is too specific or you may get bogged down in detail. For example, this is not a good way to get started: "Dr. Pellman, what are the possibilities of a meltdown occurring in a nuclear plant?"

That question may be asked later, but you would have to lead up to it. Your listeners would first have to know what is meant by a meltdown.

Do not underestimate the need for giving the qualification of the person you are talking to. It is not true that one opinion is just as good as another. Some are better than others, as when they come from better-informed people. I am more impressed by the views of a nuclear physicist on the safety of nuclear power plants than I am by those of the man on the street.

Participating in the Interview   A good interviewer will listen more than talk. However, that does not mean you should be no more than a mechanism for starting and stopping the interview. Make your presence known by injecting questions and comments at suitable times. I have heard students conducting interviews who did nothing more than introduce the guests, let them talk for five minutes, and then close out their programs. This is very burdensome to persons being interviewed. They probably do not want to talk nonstop but may do so only to keep the program from lapsing into silence. Furthermore, lacking competent guidance, they have no way of knowing whether or not they are pursuing appropriate lines of discussion. Finally, silence on the part of the host is discourteous, because it makes the guest think that the host is not listening or not interested. So do get involved in the interview. Give the respondent some feedback—something to which he or she in turn can react.

Being the respondent in an interview takes as much skill as being an interviewer. Respondents should know that it is inappropriate to talk continuously. You hope that your guest will periodically drop his or her voice and look at you as a cue to ask the next question. When this happens, be sure you are prepared with one. If it does not happen, you may have to break in. Some people continually end sentences with an upward inflection and never give you a chance to inject your own remark. This inconvenient mannerism must be countered, and there are effective ways of countering it. The most obvious is simply to pull the microphone away. (Remember that earlier we said you should never hand a microphone to the person you are interviewing.) In some cases you will each have your own microphones, however; then you will have to do something else. One way is to interrupt with a paraphrase of a point your interviewer has just made and use it as a springboard into your next question. This will make clear that you have been listening, and it will also put you back in control of the interview. In all cases, be courteous. Never interrupt a person rudely. Wait until you can do so in a manner that does not offend or appear impolite.

A different kind of problem arises where the guest is laconic. In this case you will have to carry the burden yourself. This may be difficult if you have a designated amount of time to fill. Try to figure out why the person is being quiet. It may be because you have not asked the right questions; it may be because your guest feels threatened by the microphone or by being on the air; it may be that you have given offense in some way. All you can do is try to draw the guest out. If you are unable to, keep talking yourself. If you cannot do that, close out the interview.

Asking the Questions The questions you ask will provide the direction of the interview. If the respondent is willing to follow, you can take it pretty much where you want it to go. Here is an example:

Announcer: Dr. Grant, do you see solar energy as being a workable solution to the energy crisis?
Dr. Grant: There are a number of problems. The energy has to be stored in some way, and that is expensive. To use solar energy on a large scale would require giant reflectors that take up a great deal of space. What's more, there are some politicians I could mention who oppose it because it would cut into the profit margins of the big oil, gas, and mining corporations.

Stop for a minute and consider. What would be your next question? You could pursue the point about solar energy and ask how the technical problems could be solved; you could ask what other sources of energy might be more feasible than solar energy; this would allow the respondent to set the course of the interview, at least temporarily; or you could ask about the politicians who oppose solar energy, which might lead into a whole different area of discussion. In any case, the question you ask will determine the response, and you have to make that decision very quickly.

Try to keep your questions short. Long complicated questions are difficult to understand, and you do not want to have to repeat them. The essence of the interview is the answer, so avoid detracting from it by trying to be too erudite yourself. Listen to the reply and see if the question has been properly answered. If it has not, try asking it again in a different way. If the reply still seems unresponsive, your guest may be trying to dodge it, perhaps feeling that your question was inappropriate. Do not ask questions that are too personal . . . The respondent may be very blunt in telling you that it is none of your business. This has happened on coast-to-coast radio. One of the astronauts was asked what he had said to his wife on the phone just before his takeoff. He was quite direct in his refusal to answer the question, saying that it was entirely a personal matter. Good reporting does not include prying into the intimate details of a person's private life.

When you are doing a "man-on-the-street" interview, do not ask questions that require extensive knowledge. Opinion questions are about the only ones you can ask, and even then you cannot expect much in the way of supporting evidence. You can ask people whom they are going to vote for in the presidential election, and they may be willing to tell you. But it is unfair to ask specific questions about issues that they may know little or nothing about. This kind of "public opinion poll" can add human interest to your newscast, but little in the way of enlightenment. Be careful not to let the opinions of a few people lead you to the belief that they are speaking for the larger population.

SUMMARY

Radio has become an important news medium in this country. It is not in direct competition with newspapers; the two media have different styles and purposes. The advantage of radio is its immediacy, and broadcasters should make full use of that advantage. The free press that we enjoy allows accurate and objective news reporting. The restrictions that do exist are imposed for the sake of ensuring fair play. The broadcast journalist must have a sense of responsibility and be willing to report the news as fairly and objectively as possible. The major wire services are the primary source of information for most radio stations. The copy can be read directly off the wire, but many stations choose to rewrite much of it. Newspapers and magazines can also be a source of information, but this, too, would have to be rewritten. Radio stations can subscribe to news services that provide audio feeds, so that the actual voice of the newsmaker can be heard on the air. Stations can also produce their own "actualities" by tape-recording reports and inserting actual voices into newscasts. One of a newsperson's most valuable qualifications is skill in interviewing. This is an ability that can be developed by practice and observation and one that can make a reporter a real asset to a broadcasting station.

TERMINOLOGY

Actuality
Audio feed
Jack
Lead-in
Live interview

Phone tap
Plug
Stringer
Wire service

ACTIVITIES

1 Visit your local radio station and ask the news personnel to give you some of their old teletype copy. Look through it and become familiar with the fea-

tures. Practice reading it. Compare the style of writing to that which you find in your local newspaper.

2 Find the telephone numbers of the offices and agencies listed in this chapter. Call one of the offices to get a follow-up on a story from the newspaper. Connect your phone tap to a tape recorder as described. Ask permission to record the conversation before you start asking your questions.

3 Play back the tape of the conversation that you recorded. Select the portions of it that you feel are most important. Dub those portions onto another tape recorder using the method described.

4 Write an introduction and some concluding remarks for each portion that you dubbed.

5 Record an entire newscast; use the portions of the conversations that you dubbed as actualities. Repeat the process until you can do it with confidence.

6 Listen to an interview conducted on radio or television. Evaluate in your own mind whether or not the questions were phrased clearly. Ask yourself if the respondent answered the questions directly. Was the interviewer courteous? Did the questions that were asked elicit interesting and informative answers? Did the interview hold your attention? Make a list of questions you would have asked on the same subject.

7 Have a friend or classmate read to you an article from the newspaper. As you listen, write down what you consider to be the important details. Have your friend quiz you on the article afterward. Repeat the exercise using a different article, but this time do not take notes. See how much information you can retain in your head.

8 Select a friend who has expertise in a particular area. Sit down with him or her and plan out an interview. See what questions the person would like you to ask. Agree on what the first few questions should be and, in general, what aspect of the topic you want to cover. Be sure to know the person's name and qualifications. Record the interview. Play it back for a third party and see if the questions and responses are clear and if the interview is interesting enough to hold a listener's attention.

9 Take your tape recorder to the campus center or a local coffee shop. Select a question that can be easily answered. Ask people to keep their responses short, so that you can include a variety of different voices on the tape. Using a second machine, dub a montage of answers to your question.

Chapter 13

Speaking on the Radio

BEFORE YOU SPEAK

The product of radio broadcasting is music and the spoken word. Your most important job will be to produce the words, and your basic tool is the microphone. It is not difficult to learn how to use a microphone; the hard part is knowing what to say when it is turned on. In a very few minutes almost anyone could learn how to perform the fundamental operations of a disk jockey. If you can move a switch and play a record, you qualify. But that obviously is only the first step. Being able to read copy and make interesting and informative ad lib remarks is the warp and woof of effective broadcasting.

You must learn to have confidence in front of a microphone and not be afraid of it. Speak directly into it, loud enough so that the "pot" (volume control) does not have to be set excessively high. Be sure not to start talking until you are given the cue; you are not going to be heard while the microphone is turned off. If you are operating the controls yourself, take a breath before you open your mike channel. The first sound that comes out should be the syllable of a word rather than an intake of air. And most important of all, have in mind what you are going to say, right from the start.

READING COPY

A layman may not be aware of the importance to a broadcaster of being able to read aloud effectively. Good radio or television announcers are able to read without calling attention to the pages of copy in front of them. Television broadcasters use "prompter" sheets that are placed directly under the lens of the camera, so they can look at you when they talk. Sometimes comedians make comments about the prompter sheets (commonly called "idiot cards"), but normally announcers prefer to give the effect of speaking extemporaneously. Your ability to do this will determine to a large extent whether or not you will be successful on the air.

Style

Contrary to popular belief, voice quality is not especially important. While well-modulated tones may be of some advantage, they are not essential. Style can compensate for almost any voice quality. If this were not the case, Louis Armstrong would never have succeeded as a vocalist. The style you develop is an individual thing. It must reflect an aspect of your personality, one with which you are comfortable. When you read, it is important that you be the same person you are when you speak in normal conversation. You should be able to move in and out of these two forms of communication with ease and alacrity. Much of the time you will be called upon to "ad lib around the copy."

Your style will develop over a long period of time. It will be closely tied to your personality and interests. If you are basically a serious person, your style will reflect this. You will speak in a manner that will cause people to take you seriously and believe what you say. This characteristic is called *credibility,* and it is extremely valuable to a newscaster or commentator. The "personality" disk jockey who has a fast one-liner after every record may find it difficult to establish sufficient credibility to read a newscast convincingly. Individual style is a product of many factors: rate of delivery, tone of voice, type of comment, and most of all, pacing and timing.

Pacing and Timing

These two much-used terms are difficult to define. While they may be the most important elements in oral style, they are also the most elusive. Pacing includes rate of delivery, but it refers also to variations in the rate.

In baseball a pitcher may throw a change-up to catch a batter off guard. An announcer may do the same thing: change delivery speed abruptly, to emphasize a phrase. The effectiveess of this technique is determined by the execution and by the phrase that is selected for emphasis. Timing is a close relative of pacing. It is an essential ingredient of comedy—the master of it was Jack Benny. Timing is the sense of knowing how long to "hold" on a word or a pause before picking up the next line. It is measured in fractions of seconds. The term *timing* is also used to refer to the judgment that is exercised in knowing when to say what. Anyone who has told an inappropriate joke at a party understands the importance of timing. Timing can mean knowing when to stop talking as well as when to start. Many good speeches, both on and off the air, have been ruined because they went on too long. The excessive time could be a matter of minutes or a matter of seconds.

All of the above elements, as well as many that will be mentioned later, refer to ad libbing as well as reading copy. But remember this: Almost any adult can read. There is nothing very special about that. To succeed in broadcasting you will have to set yourself apart from the millions of other people. The copy you will be called upon to read could be almost anything. Usually it will be news, commercials, public service announcements, and general station continuity.

Accuracy

It is most important to read accurately, that is, to pronounce the word that is on the page rather than another word that sounds or looks similar. It also means reading only the words on the page, and not deleting or adding words unintentionally. If the copy does not make sense you may have to change it, but this should be done *before* you go on the air. Even professionals with many years of experience are leery about reading copy "cold," without a rehearsal. If possible, take the time to actually read your copy out loud, so you can hear the sound of your own voice pronouncing the words. This will take longer than reading it silently, but the closer scrutiny usually pays off in the long run. Above all, make sure you understand what you are reading. Use a dictionary to look up meanings and correct pronunciations.

Clarity

A popular bumper sticker reads "Eschew Obfuscation" (look up the words—it's a funny line). Remember that your responsibility as a broadcaster is to clarify meaning. Avoid trying to impress people with your knowledge: Use words they can understand. And pronounce each word so that it is recognizable. Lack of clarity may be the result of mispronouncing an unfamiliar word; more often, however, it is caused by carelessness in pronouncing familiar words. Be sure to vocalize all the syllables that are supposed to be sounded in every word. Get into the habit of doing this in everyday conversation, so it will come naturally to you when you speak on the radio. An abrupt change between the way you read and the way you extemporize will be painfully apparent.

Initial Sounds A careless speaker often begins a word with the second syllable rather than the first. Do not be guilty of this. The fault most commonly occurs when a word begins with the same sound as the ending of the preceding word. "American intelligence" may come out as " 'Merican 'telligence." While the meaning may be understandable, the effect is slovenly, and the speaker is setting a poor example.

Middle Sounds The dropping of middle sounds is referred to as "telescoping" words. It happens mostly with long words, but sometimes with short ones too. "Contemplation" may become "con'umplation." It is very common to hear "prob'ly" for "probably." However, not all telescoping is incorrect. Among the British many such forms have become quite institutionalized. "Worcestershire" is properly pronounced "Woostersheer," and "halfpenny" is "hayp'ny." Closer to home, our word "extraordinary" is correctly pronounced "extrordinary." These are things that the radio announcer must come to know by using and examining the language.

Endings Dropping the endings of words is a common fault of speech. Most frequently abused is the "ing" sound. Do not say, "comin' and goin' " even if it is the articulation of middle America. However, do not overemphasize endings either. You can round off the sound so it does not appear to be an affectation.

Pronunciation

Words are the stock of the radio announcer, just as lumber and nails are the stock of the carpenter. They must be used properly. As a broadcaster you are going to be heard by hundreds or thousands of people when you talk. Your responsibility is magnified by that amount. We expect radio and television announcers to pronounce words correctly, and we will emulate them if we have nothing else to use as a standard. Network announcers who reach millions of people are especially careful about pronunciation; they know that it is not only the general public that relies on them, but that announcers in local, small-market stations do too. When I listen to the radio I don't expect announcers to be perfect, but I want them to know at least as much about the language as I do, and maybe a little more. If I feel that a speaker knows less than I do, I'll dial to another station because I want to learn something. Perhaps it is the same as it is in sports. I want to play tennis with someone who is just a little bit better than I am.

The question arises, Is pronunciation related to knowledge and intelligence? Maybe not, but it appears to be. If I hear mispronounced the name of a prominent public figure or of an often-referred-to place in the news, I lose confidence in the speaker. That attitude may not be justified, but it is there. In order to assist the announcer in establishing credibility, the news services periodically print pronunciation guides. Here is a typical one.

Figure 13-1   Pronunciation guide. *(Courtesy UPI.)*

```
-PRONUNCIATION GUIDE- (FRIDAY)

NEWS

    AMAGA, COLOMBIA -- AH-MAH-GAH'
    IDI AMIN -- ID'-EE AH-MEEN'
    MENAHEM BEGIN -- MEHN-AH'KEM BEH'-GIN
    ZULFIKAR ALI BHUTTO -- ZOOL'-FEE-KAHR AH'-LEE BOO'TOH
    BOGOTA, COLOMBIA -- BOH-GOH-TAH'
    MORARJI DESAI -- MOH-RAHR'-JEE DEH-SY'
    KENYA -- KEEN'-YUH
    HENRY KNOCHE -- NAH'KEE
    LAETRILE -- LAY'-UH-TRIHL
    HENRIETTA LEITH -- LEETH
    VALERY GISCARD D'ESTAING -- VAH-LAY-REE' ZHEES-KAHR' DEH-STANG'
    NAIROBI, KENYA -- NY-ROH'-BEE
    PANMUNJOM, KOREA --PAN-MUN-JAHM
    RAWALPINDI, PAKISTAN -- RAH-WUHL-PIN'-DEE
    ANWAR SADAT -- AHN'-WAHR SAH-DAHT'
    PIERRE TRUDEAU -- TROO-DOH'
    ZIA UL-HAQ -- ZEE UHL-HAHK
```

People knowledgeable in some fields are more critical than those in others. Classical music buffs are perhaps the most critical of all. You should know how to pronounce the names of these frequently heard composers. The pronunciation guide is in slightly different form from the one used by the wire services, but it is one that you will often see used in broadcast scripts.

Figure 13-2 Composers.

```
Johann Sebastian Bach (YO-hahn Seh-bahs-tiahn Bahkh)
Wolfgang Amadeus Mozart (VOHLF-gong Ah-mah-DAY-oos MOAT-sart)
Richard Wagner (REE-khard VAHG-ner)
Ludwig van Beethoven (LOOD-vig vahn BAY-toe-vn)
Franz Joseph Haydn (Frahnts YO-zef HIGH-dn)
Giuseppe Verdi (Joo-ZEP-eh VAIR-dee)
Giacomo Puccini (JA-ko-mo Poo-CHEE-nee)
Franz Schubert (Frahnts SHOE-beart)
Carl Maria von Weber (Karl Ma-REE-ah fun VAY-bear)
Felix Mendelssohn (FAY-lix MEND-l-sohn)
Frederic Chopin (Fray-day-REEK Show-PAN)
Edvard Grieg (Ed-vard GREEG)
Antonin Dvorak (AHN-toneen Duh-VOR-zhock)
Peter Tchaikovsky (Peter Chi-KOFF-ski)
Igor Stravinsky (EE-gor Strah-VIN-ski)
Hector Berlioz (Eck-tor BEAR-lee-oz)
Claude Debussy (Clohde Duh-Beu-SEE)
```

Now try pronouncing these names of works by famous composers.

Figure 13-3 Musical works.

```
Peer Gynt Suite (Pair Gint Sweet)
Die Fledermaus (Dee FLAY-der-mouse)
La Traviata (Lah Trah-vee-AH-ta)
La Bohème (Lah Bo-EHM)
Eine Kleine Nachtmusik (EYE-neh KLY-neh NAHKHT-moo-zeek)
Capriccio Espagnol (Kah-PREACH-ee-o Es-Pahn-YOLE)
Le Coq D'Or Suite (Luh Cuk-DOOR Sweet)
Die Walküre (Dee VAHL-cure-eh)
Aïda (Eye-EE-duh)
Largo Al Factotum (Largo Ahl Fahk-TOE-tum)
```

Common words may give you as much difficulty as hard-to-pronounce names. This is especially true when the words are similar to other words.

accept—except   affect—effect
access—excess   amplitude—aptitude
adapt—adopt   are—our

Arthur—author	line—lion
ascent—accent	lose—loose
climatic—climactic	Mongol—mongrel
comprise—compromise	morning—mourning
consecrate—confiscate	pictures—pitchers
consolation—consultation	sex—sects
disillusion—dissolution	statue—statute
exit—exist	vocation—vacation
immorality—immortality	wandered—wondered[1]

Some words are mispronounced because of the combination of sounds in sequence. Try these tongue twisters:

> The existentialist called for specific statistics.
> The President set a precedent for preserving precipitant performance.

Be careful not to interchange the "pre" sound and the "per" sound. P's and S's can be particularly troublesome because they tend to pop and hiss on a microphone. Try not to hit the P too hard or extend the S too long.

Placing the accent in the proper place can be another problem. Use a dictionary to find the correct pronunciation for each of the following words:

abdomen	contractor	hospitable	resources
acclimated	despicable	inquiry	robust
admirable	dirigible	irrefutable	romance
aspirant	exquisite	pretense	theater
autopsy	finance	recess	vehement[2]
comparable	grimace	research	

Emphasis

One of the important principles in the study of semantics is that *words are not containers of meaning.* In the English language there are over 750,000 words. All but a few of them have not one but several meanings. Therefore, meaning is contained in the speaker or the writer—not in the words. Words are the tools we use to communicate, and their meaning can be altered by the way we use them. For example, the meaning of a sentence can be changed if the emphasis is shifted from one word to another. How is this done? Consider first the devices used by writers.

---

[1] John P. Moncur and Harrison M. Karr, *Developing Your Speaking Voice,* 2d ed. (New York: Harper & Row, 1972), p. 226.
[2] Ibid.

They can put a word in CAPITAL LETTERS; they can underline or *use italics;* they can use punctuation such as quotation marks or exclamation marks. Announcers, of course, cannot use these, but they can use *vocal inflection.* They can utilize change in volume, pitch, or rate of delivery. See if you can alter the meaning of the following sentence by modifying the stress that you place on the words:

I can change meaning by emphasizing important words.

Vocal Inflection

Vocal inflection is important for two reasons: (1) It helps to hold the interest of the listener, and (2) it helps to communicate accurately what you mean. Meaning must be considered at the *affective* as well as the *cognitive* level. In other words, the *emotional mood* that you set will influence the *intellectual meaning* of the communication. An announcer must be sensitive enough to know when to adopt a serious, concerned tone of voice and to be able to *project* that *feeling* in speech. For example, a news item that describes a tragic event should not be read in the same analytical tone that one would use when reading a stock market report. It is, of course, inappropriate for an announcer to become overly emotional or maudlin when describing a tragedy, but it should be apparent to the listener that the announcer is a human being and has feelings like anyone else.

Achieving the appropriate degree of vocal inflection is not easy. People tend to speak in a monotone when they are talking casually to friends. Vocal inflection reveals emotions, and some individuals are reluctant to permit that. It may also be that strong vocal inflection is not necessary when you are standing very close to a person and can see facial expression and physical posture. But an audience can not see the face of the announcer; the communication comes only through the auditory sense. *There is no body language in radio.* Your entire message must come through the cone of a loudspeaker. Everything you *mean* must be *heard.*

Radio and television are mass media because messages are received simultaneously by large numbers of people. However, the announcer must not speak as though addressing a large group. Broadcasting is intimate in that the listener is not aware of the existence of the multitude of other listeners. As far as the listener is concerned, the voice on the radio is speaking to him or her alone. The listener expects to be treated as one unique person, not to be addressed in the plural, as if by a public speaker facing a large audience. An exception to this occurs when the President

Figure 13-4 Talking to the radio audience.

addresses the nation. In this case listeners know they are hearing a prepared speech, and that each person is one of a large group. But even
then, Presidents are inclined to use the less formal phrase, "my friends"
or "my fellow Americans," rather than "ladies and gentlemen." When
some announcers broadcast they will picture in their minds one person
to represent the type of audience the station hopes to reach. It could be
a man commuting to work, a woman working in the home, or a teenager
coming home from school. If you read your copy to that person as
though he or she were in the same room with you, you will have a good
chance of achieving the kind of communication that reaches a large
number of people in the same category. The best radio announcers are
friendly, informal, sincere, and intimate.

Rate

One of the factors of style is your rate of delivery. Students frequently
ask me how fast they should talk. The answer is, no faster than is comfortable and fast enough to hold the interest of the audience. The rate, of
course, will vary depending upon what you are reading, but in general I
would suggest you talk as fast as you can without slurring or telescoping

words or interfering with your vocal inflection. Consider this: Under laboratory conditions some people can comprehend an oral message that is played back on a tape recorder as fast as 400 words per minute—much faster than anyone can talk. Normally you speak at a rate of about 125 to 160 words per minute. This means that, while you are talking, the listener's mind can be engaged in other matters. Probably it is flitting from one thing to another every few seconds. You are only one of a number of stimuli competing for attention. If you speak too slowly, you are leaving enough time to focus on something else. Your listener may get the meaning of your sentence before you are through saying it, and then allow her or his mind to wander away. The copy you are reading out loud could be read silently by the listener in a fraction of the time it takes you to say it. So justify the time that the listener spends with you. Remember that the listener is in complete control and can turn you off at any time.

Volume

How loud should you talk? Certainly there is no need to shout because microphone output can be amplified to any level necessary. However, remember that as you turn up the gain, you also pick up more ambient noise. Project the voice. Keep in mind that a certain minimum amount of vocal output is necessary for effective vocal inflection. The volume you use in everyday conversation may therefore not be sufficient for radio announcing. Again, remember that your message is filtered through a speaker cone. Your listeners can not see your lips move; nor can they observe the expression on your face. They get the meaning only from the sound of the words. Furthermore, they are not sitting with their ears glued to the speaker. Usually people are doing other things while they listen. If they are in a car, your message has to compete with the noise of traffic; at home the radio a person is listening to may be in the next room. What you say has to penetrate distance, inattention, and interference. With all this you may wonder if anybody will understand you at all.

AD LIBBING

Most of what was said in the preceding section on reading copy also applies to ad libbing—a broadcaster's term meaning to extemporize or to speak impromptu. Whether you are speaking from copy or without it, your articulation and enunciation must be clear enough so that you can be understood. At the same time it must be *natural*. Even though radio announcing is a lot of work and requires a good deal of preparation, you have to make it sound easy. The listener should not be able to perceive any strain or tension in your voice. Regardless of how much effort you put into writing your script or preparing your ad libs, your remarks should sound spontaneous, as if they were just welling up from within you. The fact that so many good announcers sound this way is deceptive. It tends to make one think that a beginner can sit down and do the same thing with no effort or preparation. It may seem like a contradiction in terms when I say that your ad libs should be prepared, but that is exactly what they should be. Most ad lib comments have been thought about in advance—sometimes even written down. Entertainers with many years of experience can rely on their wits, but they have much background to call upon.

Most of your ad libbing you will do as a disk jockey between records. Probably the station you work for will have a policy about how much you should talk—and maybe even what you should say. A station may want you to talk after every record, or they may want you to play a "set" of two or three records. There may be specific times when you are to give time signals and weather reports. There may also be catch phrases or slogans prepared for you, to promote the station. Very likely there will be guidelines for the length of time you are to talk. Usually it is short—and for a good reason. It is very difficult to sustain audience attention with an extended ad lib. You are not being paid as an entertainer. If there is humor in your remarks, it must be direct, succinct, and to the point. Some station managers say, "be a personality, but do it in not more than twenty seconds."

Most disk jockeys would like to talk more than they are allowed to, but some that I have known feel that any talk is an imposition on the listener. If you fall into the second category, consider this: Those who want *only* music will buy phonographs and maybe even eight-track tape players for their cars. People who listen to the radio do so because they want to hear talk as well as music. Talk is not an imposition; the voice on the air is company for someone who is alone. It also provides information and entertainment. If talk were not valuable and desirable, it would have been dropped from broadcasting long ago. The important thing is to take a *positive attitude* toward what you say. Do not feel that you have to apologize for interrupting the music. You must be able to believe that the commercial or the public service announcement you are reading or talking about is important and that some people will listen to it and act upon what you tell them. Remember that your job is to *sell* the product, whether it be used cars, the United Crusade, or your own radio station.

Reading what is written for you is one thing, but how do you ad lib effectively? There is no easy answer. It will depend largely upon your own personality and interests. For the most part, disk jockeys talk about the records they are playing. So the first requisite is for you to know something about your artists and their music. The second is to choose such bits from the information you have as will make good ad lib remarks. Probably no one can prescribe a formula. All the rules can be, and are, broken by professionals once they get established. But here are a few guidelines that may prove helpful for the beginner:

1 *Do not use broadcast jargon.* Speak in language that is generally understood by the public rather than in technical terms. If you say you are operating *combo* and watching your *VU meter,* nobody is going to know what you are talking about.

2 *Avoid using trite phrases repeatedly.* It is easy to fall into the habit of relying on trite phrases, but their repeated use is annoying. A few examples are "Let's see now . . ."; "You know . . ."; and "Here's a little bit of. . . ." These expressions are just fillers that people utter while they are thinking of what they really want to say. Your talk will be greatly enhanced if you leave them out.

3 *Do not carry on private conversations with someone in the control room.* Have your fun, but let the audience in on it too. If something happens that makes you laugh, tell the rest of us about it. We'll feel left out otherwise. A certain amount of this sort of cutting up may be all right, but don't let it go too far. Some station managers will say not to let it happen at all.

4 *Do not sell yourself or the station too hard.* Resist the temptation of telling the listeners what a great show you have and what a marvelous station it is. Let them decide that for themselves. Repeating your own name or the call letters of the station after every record gets very tiresome.

5 *Avoid anticlimactic words and phrases at the end of your ad lib.* All too often the beginner (and sometimes the "old pro") fails to recognize the appropriate end of the ad lib and adds a phrase or two that ruins the effect. It is the same as trying to explain a joke after you have told it— the impact is lost. To avoid this, have your hand on the switch that starts the next record before you finish your remark. Hit the music at the climax of your ad lib. If they don't get it, there is nothing you can do about it.

6 *Do not be negative about any announcement you read or any program you put on the air.* If there is a commercial or a public service announcement you dislike, talk to the program director about it privately, but never put it down on the air. Remember that someone had a good reason for scheduling it. Your job is to sell it. A program you introduce may not be to your taste, but it is entitled to the same respect as any other item on the schedule.

7 *Do not use offensive language.* Obscenity on the air is a violation of the penal code and of the *Rules and Regulations* of the Federal Communications Commission. However, other forms of offensive speech are to be avoided as well. Ethnic slurs and crude jokes have no place on the airwaves either.

Most of the restrictions are matters of common sense.

What to Talk About

What kind of ad lib remarks *do* meet the test of good broadcast practice? Aside from comments about the records and the weather, what does a disk jockey talk about?

1 *Coming events.* This is perhaps the most valuable service a disk jockey can provide. No one expects to hear anything particularly profound on the radio these days—at least not on an everyday basis. But they would like to know what is going on. In a minute or less you can tell about an event that is coming up in the listening territory, giving most of the vital information. This is an area where the disk jockey should be well informed. He or she should have broad enough interests to talk about a variety of subjects. Movies, plays, sporting events, lectures, college courses, festivals, rodeos, dog shows—all are activities that would be of interest to someone. Sit down and make a list of all the public places you can think of in your broadcast area. Then set about to learn what is happening at each place. This alone will give you plenty to talk about.

2 *Current events.* The bulk of the news will probably be covered on the regularly scheduled newscasts, but there are always features and human interest items that you can talk about. Your comments need not be lengthy—better that they not be. Just a short reference, to pique the curiosity, will suffice. Read the newspaper every day as a matter of course. In addition, subscribe to a current events magazine. Talk to people about the news. You will find yourself making ad lib remarks on the air that were tried out first in conversation with your friends.

3 *Current trends and fashions.* A radio announcer should be abreast of the avant-garde. People are interested in new things that are happening even if they have no wish to become actively involved. As the purveyor of this information you are not necessarily an advocate. The trends you talk about may be streaking, transcendental meditation, or goldfish swallowing—all of which were new at one time. They may also be academically or scientifically oriented topics such as behavior modification, artificial intelligence, or the DNA molecule. You need not be an expert on these subjects. But when they come up, you should have a nodding acquaintance with them and be able to make some response.

4 *Sports and recreation.* Next to the weather, the subject most likely to be a common denominator of audience interest is sports. People who never listen to the news often will be very attentive to comments about their favorite baseball or football team. They may also want to know how the fishing is in certain areas or what the snow conditions are like during ski season.

5 *Books, plays, and movies.* You may not want to set yourself up as a critic—and that would be hard to do in a minute or less—but you can make brief comments about new books, movies, and plays. There is so much that is published and shown these days that people are grateful for some guidance as to what is worth reading or attending. Your opinion, even if not the final word, does give the public something to go on. In your spare time be sure you do more than watch television—everyone does that. Read as much as you can, and find out what is going on outside your own home.

Assuming that you have followed the above suggestions, had the experiences, and acquired the information—how do you work any of these things into your show? You may be able to tie it in to something you are doing on the air, to the music you have played or an announcement you have just read. Perhaps there is a relationship to the topic of a guest speaker you have had or will have on your program. Or you may just have to bring it up cold. Once the subject has been introduced, you can make periodic references to it between records. This will give some continuity to what you are doing. A word of caution, however: Do not assume that your listeners have been following your commentary right from the very beginning. Tailor your remarks so that anyone can pick them up from any point along the way and be able to make sense out of them. One of the reasons radio soap operas were so successful was that a listener could tune in any day and in a very short time be able to piece the story together. The writing was skillful enough to conceal the needed repetitiveness. Another feature of the "soaps" was that there were always several story lines running concurrently. You are not obliged to stay on the same subject throughout your program. You can develop several themes simultaneously.

The chief requirement for success in broadcasting is that you be an interesting person. Fortunately, while you are being interesting to other people you are being interesting to yourself as well.

SUMMARY

The most demanding task in radio broadcasting is knowing what to say when the microphone is turned on. The professional announcer or combo operator must be able to ad lib as well as read copy clearly and accurately. Style and timing are important attributes—as is correct pronunciation and enunciation. The voice that is transmitted must penetrate noise and other sounds that compete for the attention of the listener. The words must be clear and well modulated. Even more important, the professional announcer must have something to say that is either informative or entertaining. Almost anyone has the ability to close a microphone switch and start talking. Being a professional broadcaster requires more than that.

TERMINOLOGY

Ad lib	Project
Enunciation	Pronunciation
Extemporize	Set
Initial sounds	Telescoping
Middle sounds	Timing
Pacing	Vocal inflection

ACTIVITIES

1 Read the paragraph below into a tape recorder. Play it back to yourself and check your pronunciation and enunciation. Are all the syllables clearly sounded? Are you putting stress on the words that need to be highlighted? Are you able to make it sound natural and spontaneous? Are the proper names pronounced correctly?

> Good evening. Our concert this evening will begin with the Peer Gynt Suites numbers one and two by Edvard Grieg performed by the Boston Pops orchestra, Arthur Fiedler conducting. Then we will hear Mozart's *Eine Kleine Nachtmusik,* and finally selections from the opera *Die Walküre* by Richard Wagner. May we remind you that tomorrow night our featured work will be the New World Symphony by Antonin Dvorak. Our opera selections will include excerpts from Verdi's *Aïda* and Puccini's *La Bohème.* Here now is the first of the Peer Gynt Suites.

> Play the tape for someone who is familiar with classical music and see if there are any mistakes in your pronunciation.

2 The following sentences were written to include words that have sound-alikes. Speak the sentences into your tape recorder; play back the tape and see if the words are clearly distinguished.

> Accept the fact that everyone is right except you.
> If you cannot adapt to changes, you must adopt a new philosophy.
> The climatic conditions may be anticlimactic.
> The diplomat attempted to comprise a compromise.
> The dissolution of the marriage may lead to disillusion.
> The exit does exist.
> The sects performed rites of sex.
> There is a statute against defacing a statue.

Chapter 14

Finding a Job

THE SMALL-MARKET STATION

When you are first breaking into radio, your best opportunities are in the small-market areas. Cities with populations of 30,000 or less are regarded as small market. Little 250-watt stations in rural communities can be a lot of fun, and they provide excellent experience for the beginning broadcaster. Programming is generally fairly loose, with much greater variety than you will find in the metropolitan areas. Small stations may be more receptive to your ideas and might allow you to do a children's program or a man-on-the-street report. Frequently the small-market station will carry such things as Little League baseball games and live music from the Grange Hall. You may not make much money, but you will learn much and enjoy radio more than you will doing a tight format in a major market.

A college station can also give you good experience. It is one place where you can experiment without having to worry about losing sponsors or getting fired if your ratings drop. Moreover, you will get a chance to do every job there is in radio if you are willing to take advantage of the opportunity. At a college station you may be able to determine some of the programming, set the schedules, keep the logs, contact record distributors, work on promotion, and perhaps even do some of the maintenance. If you play a musical instrument, speak a foreign language, or have some other performing talent, the college station can provide you with an audience.

If you have gotten this far in the book, you are probably interested enough to consider broadcasting seriously. Begin thinking about what you can do to make yourself employable.

1 Get a restricted permit or third class license. Better still, get a second or even a first class license.

2 Get on-the-air experience at a noncommercial, college or community station. Learn to operate the equipment smoothly and efficiently.

3 Learn to type, and practice writing copy. Start by composing public service announcements; then begin writing news.

4 Be able to read aloud accurately and without stumbling. Develop the ability to use voice inflection to communicate the idea.

5 Practice interviewing. Learn to extract answers from knowledgeable people by asking concise, well-phrased questions.

6 Expand your vocabulary. Master unfamiliar words. Learn to use the pronunciation guide in the dictionary. Practice a few new words every night.

7 Listen to music. All kinds. Become familiar with titles, artists, and composers in as many musical areas as you can handle.

8 Read newspapers, current magazines, and books. Become a critic of movies, plays, and television shows.

9 Finish college. If you do not actually get a degree, at least take courses that will introduce you to the arts, sciences, and humanities. Develop an appreciation for all aspects of culture.

10 Read up on FCC *Rules and Regulations.* Become familiar with the laws under which you will be working.

11 Learn something about electronics. Be able to read meters, solder a wire, and understand the language of the chief engineer.

12 Get some experience in sales. If nothing else, do some door-to-door selling. Learn what it is like to make a dozen or more calls before making a sale.

When you have done these things you are ready to start looking for a job.

PREPARE A RESUME

Your résumé should be an accurate reflection of your professional capabilities. It is your attention-getting device, your foot-in-the-door. It should be brief but at the same time reveal whatever a prospective employer ought to know about your competence. When preparing a résumé, do not be modest. It is no time to hide your light under a bushel. It is a chance for you to set down in the record the things you have done and the experiences you have had that are really valuable and contribute to your professional stature.

The Basic Information

Include all the information the employer will need to get in touch with you. Your name, address (with zip code), and telephone number. Also give your age, your marital status, and the condition of your health. Indicate how soon you would be available; if you are working, you will want to give your employer two weeks' notice. Tell what license you hold, and give the expiration date. If you have a college or university degree, say when and where you received it.

Professional Goals

Tell what job or jobs you are applying for and what type of work you are qualified to do. Put down only the jobs you are willing to accept. If you do not want a typist's job, leave that out. Also there is no need to restrict yourself to the job titles that already exist at the station. It is entirely possible to create a job for yourself by identifying a need that the station has. For example, the station may not have a public affairs director. If you are the right person at the right time, the station may make a place for you. You may want to contact a station that goes off the air at midnight and persuade them to run an all-night show. (Your position will be stronger if you are able to suggest several sponsors willing to buy time during that period.) It can be helpful for the management to know whether you are a "morning person" or a "night person," so specify the time period you feel best suits you.

Work Experience

Normally this would include radio stations for which you have worked. But if you are just starting, you will have to list other experience. If you have been working at a college or community station be sure to list that, even though you were not being paid. Be specific about the number of hours you worked, the kind of equipment you operated, and the type of work you did.

Other kinds of work could be included in this section as well— preferably that which is related to broadcasting, but almost anything will help. Employers want to know whether or not you have the "work ethic." They want to know if you can persevere and stick to a job, even though it may become routine. In almost every case they will choose to employ a steady, dependable worker that they know they can count on, over the "hotshot" who may or may not show up. So your résumé should attempt to demonstrate that you are this dependable kind of person. I would suggest that you not list jobs that you held for only a short period of time, or those in which you had a personality conflict with the employer. It is quite possible that previous employers will be solicited for references.

Do list volunteer work you have done that is in any way related to the broadcasting field. Incidentally, you might think about doing volunteer work specifically for the sake of acquiring experience to include on a résumé. That is an excellent way to get started. Offer your services to a nonprofit organization and see if you can work in their public relations department. You could make yourself very valuable writing public service announcements for radio stations and news releases for the local papers. In this way you get experience and at the same time make contacts that could prove to be helpful when you start applying for a job.

Academic Background

Start with your most recent degree if you have one. Then, in reverse order, include any other colleges you have attended and course work you have done. Be sure to state your major and the specific courses taken that relate to broadcasting. Name the high school from which you were graduated, but not the elementary school.

Cocurricular Activities

Course work is not the only valuable experience to be gained in college and high school. You will certainly want to mention activities that you pursued and offices that you held. Here again, this is something to think about while you are in college. Active participation in student government, clubs, sports, and social functions not only contributes to your personal growth but makes you a more attractive job candidate as well.

Hobbies and Interests

If there is anything that you are not able to work into the other sections you can include it here. Such hobbies as amateur radio operation or other work in electronics would certainly be relevant. "Interests" might include playing a musical instrument or doing magic shows at birthday parties. While these talents in themselves would not be enough to get you a job, one of them might just strike the right chord in the mind of the station manager and make your application stand out from the others. I know one young man who claims he got his job because he knew how to juggle.

The résumé should be neatly typed and prepared in outline form. Generally speaking, it should not be more than two pages. It is not supposed to be a comprehensive description of all aspects of your personality; it is designed only to get you a personal interview. If it accomplishes that, you can consider it to have been successful. Make several copies of the résumé, update it periodically, and have it on hand whenever an opportunity arises. Figure 14-1 is an example of a résumé that you can use as a model.

MAKE AN AUDITION TAPE

When you apply for a job, some stations will request that you send them an audition tape. This is a sample of the work that you can be expected to do if you get the job. The best idea is to tailor your audition tape for the station to which you are applying. That way you can use their call letters and play the kind of music that is consistent with their policy. But this is not absolutely necessary. You can make one tape and send out copies to several stations as long as there are not vast differences in their programming styles. Use a small roll of reel-to-reel tape of fairly good quality. Do not expect to get it back.

In order to make an acceptable audition tape you will have to have access to professional equipment. If you are taking a broadcasting course in college, the equipment available to you there should be adequate. The tape should represent the best work you are able to produce. Avoid putting yourself in the position of having to make excuses for it. Follow these important basic rules:

1 *Bulk-erase the tape before you start.* Do not take the chance of having your tape cluttered up with previously recorded material.

2 *Keep it short.* Probably not more than 2 or 3 minutes of it will be listened to. The first 30 seconds are critical, so be sure to get off to a good start. Otherwise the rest of the tape may not be heard at all.

3 *If you use a stereo recorder, record on the left track or on both tracks; never on the right track alone.* A recording made on the right track of a stereo recorder will not play back at all on some (half-track) mono machines.

4 *Be sure the tape is clearly identified.* Put your name on the box

```
                        RESUME

Robert J. Smith             Age:  24
847 Columbus Avenue         Birthdate:  August 30, 1954
Sunnyvale, California 94086
                            3rd Class Radiotelephone
Phone:  (408) 555-1212      Operator's Permit


Available on two weeks' notice   Marital status:  Single
Salary expected:  Union scale    Health:  Good
             *******************************
Professional Goals

I would like to do on-the-air work for an AM or FM radio station.  I
am familiar with a variety of styles of music, particularly top 40
and progressive rock.  I also have knowledge of folk music and some
country-western.  I can operate combo and am familiar with basic
broadcast audio equipment.  In addition to disk-jockey work I can also
qualify as a newscaster.  I can write copy and can type 35 words per
minute.

Work Experience

KSAN                        June 1977 to Sept. 1977.  Record filing and
345 Sansome                 general organizing of materials for on-the-
San Francisco, Calif.       air personnel.  Some copy writing and pro-
                            duction assistance. (Part time for college
                            credit)


KFJC                        Sept. 1975 to June 1977.  On-the-air work
Foothill College            as disk jockey and newscaster.  Copy writer
Los Altos Hills, Calif.     for public service announcements.  Served
                            on management staff as Public Service Dir-
                            ector for four months (Part time)

Baskin-Robbins Ice          June 1976 to Sept. 1976.  Behind-the-counter
Cream Store                 sales work.  Operation of cash register.
267 University Avenue       (Full time)
Palo Alto, Calif.

Academic Background

Foothill College            Graduate-AA Degree, 1977.  Major: Broadcasting.
Los Altos Hills,            Coursework included:  Radio station operation;
Calif.                      Broadcast journalism;  Speech;  Television
                            production.

Sunnyvale High School       Graduate-June 1972.
Sunnyvale, Calif.

Co-Curricular Activities

        Debate team         Sunnyvale High School from 1971 to 1972.
                            Participated in three tournaments.  Also at
                            Foothill College 1976 to 1977.  Attended
                            two tournaments and several on-the-air debates.

        Speakers' bureau    Sunnyvale High School, 1972.  Participated
                            in Lions Club Speech Contest.

Hobbies and Interests

        Music               I have been interested in music all my life. I
                            have a collection of over 1,000 records; I play
                            the guitar and sing.  I attend concerts and am
                            familiar with the current performers and their music.

        Sports              I prefer participating in sports rather than
                            being a spectator.  I ski, play tennis, and swim.
```

Figure 14-1 Résumé.

and on the tape reel itself. Also, give your name on the tape when you start to record. You can say, "This is Bob Smith auditioning for KLOK." Or you can simply use your name in your ad lib remarks.

   5 *Telescope the music.* The person listening to the tape wants to hear what *you* sound like, not what the music sounds like. Ad lib into a record, play the first few bars of the music, and stop the tape recorder. Move the needle over to the end of the selection, and then start your recorder again. On playback the listener will hear only about ten seconds of the music but will hear your remarks at the beginning and at the end.

6 *Ad lib and read copy.* The two kinds of radio announcing are reading and ad libbing. In order to work on the air, you have to do both of these well. Many stations require their disk jockeys to read news, so your tape should demonstrate that as well as your proficiency in reading spot announcements.

The list above includes the basic features of any audition tape. You should bear in mind that several other people will certainly be applying for the job you would like to get. How are you going to make your audition tape stand out from all the others? Are you more entertaining than those other people? More credible? Are you giving more information? Is your timing better? Is your voice quality superior? Do you have a style that fits in with that of the station? It is very difficult to second guess what a station manager or program director is looking for. They may not know themselves, only that they recognize it when they hear it. But somehow you will have to give them a reason for selecting you over the competition. The decision may actually be made on factors other than your vocal delivery; there probably are dozens of people who sound just as good on the air as you do. But that certainly is not the only factor that managers will consider. Other skills, such as writing, will be very much to your advantage. Along with your résumé, include some copy that you have written. You may even want to read that copy on your audition tape. Production work is also a factor that station managers will take into account. If you have produced a spot announcement that includes sound and music under voice, send that along, either separately or as a part of your audition tape. Make sure the prospective employer is aware of the special talents that you have.

LOOKING FOR A JOB

The job market in broadcasting varies just as it does in any other industry. Jobs are generally more prevalent when business is good and the economy is expanding. During recession periods people tend to hang onto their jobs more tightly, and there are fewer openings available. But in general, a characteristic of the broadcasting industry is its fluidity. People tend to move around a lot. There are opportunities for beginners, if you are willing to look for them. There are several things you have to understand:

1 *You must be willing to move.* There are jobs available, but probably not in your home town. The best opportunities are in the small-market areas. The pay may not be good, but the experience will be excellent.

2 *Working conditions may not be the best.* You have to love being on the air in order for the job to be worthwhile. You may have to work a split shift, and perhaps a 6-day week. Rather than working in the downtown studios, you may be assigned to the transmitter site which could be located in the middle of a cornfield or a swamp.

3 *You may not get the job of your choice.* Beginners sometimes fail to get employment because they confine their job search to their own favorite stations. You can not afford to be this particular. Apply at whatever station has an opening. You do not have to regard the job you take as being a lifetime post. Plan on working at several stations; that is the nature of the industry.

While it is perfectly permissible to apply to any station for a job, your efforts will be more fruitful if you have some way of discovering where the openings are. One way is to look in the trade journals. The magazine *Broadcasting,* for example, has a classified section which always lists a variety of jobs available all over the country. There are other agencies such as *Job Leads* that also provide information about job opportunities.

BECOMING A BROADCASTER

You may feel that being a disk jockey is the greatest job in the world. You may possibly continue to feel that way for several years. Certainly there are people who do become so successful at it that the job does become a lifetime career. But most people who go into the broadcasting business are disk jockeys only for a relatively short period of time. There are reasons for this, many of which we have mentioned in earlier chapters. For one thing there is very little job security, even in the large metropolitan markets. Highly paid disk jockeys with many years of experience frequently get fired for a variety of reasons—their ratings drop, the station changes hands, their material begins to get stale, or the management just wants to take a fresh approach. Getting fired is painful under any circumstances. But it is particularly difficult when you have a family to support and a mortgage to pay. This is why people in the broadcasting business, as they get older, tend to look for positions in the field that offer a bit more security. You are not going to be a disk jockey all your life. If you have not found a fairly secure spot by the time you are 30, try some other business.

Job Leads

VOLUME VIII, NUMBER 12   APRIL 9, 1979   THE WEEKLY MEDIA EMPLOYMENT NEWSLETTER

Help Wanted

RADIO ANNOUNCERS

MORNING DRIVE DJ needed for this Top 40/Disco station. Some experience preferred. More important, though, "is how it sounds on tape." Rush tape and resume to John McCloud, KLIV, Box 995, San Jose, CA 95108. No calls, please.

NIGHT JOCK. Experience is preferred for this slot. T & R to Mike Farrow, WCRO, 605 Main, Johnstown, PA 15901. No calls.

NO FIRST-TIMERS for the mid-day slot at this Adult Contemporary station. Production background required. You'll handle a lot of remotes and personal appearances. Call or mail T & R to Pete Gabriel, WKBN, 3920 Sunset, Youngstown, PA 44501. (216) 782-1144.

TOP FORTY outlet wants a morning drive person. You may send your T & R, but they'd prefer to talk to you by phone first: Darrell Ward, KCRS, Box 4607, Midland, TX 79701. (915) 563-0550.

BREAK IN on the midnight - 6 am shift and move up from there. Need Third endorsed and good voice to work for this Contemporary outlet. Once you prove yourself on this shift, you can move to another slot at this 24-hour operation. Shag Miller, KBOW / KOPR, 660 Dewey Blvd., Butte, MT 59701. Miller tells us: "We used Job Leads last November with excellent results. We hired two of the applicants; one of whom was forced to leave because of family circumstances and the other has been promoted to another air shift at our station."

MOR ANNOUNCER with strong production skills. You'll work a five day week, Wednesday -Sunday. Three years of MOR background required, and automation helpful. $250/week. No calls. T & R to Mahlon Moore, WNOG Radio, 333 Eighth Street South, Naples, FL 33940.

OHIO FM has an immediate opening for an experienced announcer to handle a limited airshift and heavy production. Automation. "Excellent pay and benefits." Write Bob Mc-Lyman, WNDH, Box 111, Napoleon, OH 43545 or call Bob or Dick, (419) 592-8060.

TWO POSITIONS open at this highly-rated adult MOR station in the beautiful Monterey Bay area. One will take the morning shift, and the other shift is not yet certain. Experience with production skills preferred—not really for beginners. Call or send tape and resume to Ken Cooper, Operations Director, KESE, Box 2108, Monterey, CA 93940. (408) 373-1236.

AIR TALENT needed for this Top 40 station. Heavy production responsibilities. You must be experienced. Ray Brown, WCOD, 105 Stevens Street, Hyannis, MA 02601.

WINX has an immediate opening for a fulltime AM drive announcer with a mature voice and informative approach (not just music). Send resume, tape and salary requirements to Box 1726, Rockville, MD 20850.

NIGHT TIME announcer for Country Music show. You should be familiar with Country format and have at least two years of experience. Salary negotiable. Contact James E. Ragsdale, Personnel Director-Broadcasting, Box 100, Nashville, TN 37202. WSM Radio.

MORNING ANNOUNCER with a strong personality. This Contemporary/MOR wants someone with a lot of community involvement. T & R to Mark Hayes, KPRL Radio, Box 7, Paso Robles, CA 93446.

WARM, MATURE announcer for top-rated easy listening station. Job Leads is told this is "not traditional Beautiful Music. We do remotes, special events." Ability is more important than education or experience, "but that doesn't mean that we're not willing to pay for someone good." 40-hour week. T & R to Rick MacNamara, WHEZ, 3570 Skyview Drive, Huntington, WV 25701. You may call, but not collect: (304) 529-2558.

TWO WITH A FIRST: This Illinois outlet wants to improve its sound, and needs two air talents with First Phones to do it. Looking for 3- 4 years of experience—no beginners... Contemporary Oldies. Call or mail T & R to Jon Morgan, 1215 Fern Avenue, St. Charles, IL 60174. (312) 584-1483. This address and number updates earlier incorrect listing in Job Leads.

PD & ANNOUNCERS needed for town of 30,000 in New Mexico. New Adult Contemporary has excellent facilities. You should have some experience—but talent more important. Bob Tate, 1328 Coffee, Number One, Pampa TX 79065. (806) 669-7012.

WHY NOT TRY a 10 - 2 pm airshift plus substantial local news duties. Some production. Try the fresh air about as far north as you can go and still be in California. Dave Stevens says the opening is immediate at this Contemporary with mass appeal. And Dave wouldn't lie to you. After all, he got HIS job through Job Leads, and would like to keep the tradition alive. Give him a call or rush your tape and resume to KPOD, Drawer Q, Crescent City, CA 95531. (707) 464-3183.

ANNOUNCER / SALES for expanding radio stations. "Excellent starting salary with good future," says the boss. If you're the man or woman for this one, call A. Dresner or write WELV Radio, Box 309, Ellenville, NY 12428. (914) 647-5678.

CALIFORNIA NEEDS a six-day announcer who is flexible as to format. You'll work 6 pm - midnight five days, and noon to 6 pm on Saturday. The ideal candidate will be "a personable communicator" who can read, handle some news and some talk. The format in this slot is currently rock—but Job Leads has learned that it may be shifting soon. So if all you can do is scream into a microphone, you're probably not the one for this job. Call or mail T & R to Beth Quigley, KLOA, Box 938, Ridgecrest, CA 93555. (714) 375-8888.

NEW CONTEMPORARY outlet needs a production person who's creative with tape and might be interested in sales. Experience preferred. No calls, please. Send T & R to b Carson, Carson Communications, 1145 Willora, Stockton, CA 95207.

PART-TIME weekend DJ needed who will also do work during expanded summer programming. They would like person to have some experience, plus 3rd, but will do training. You won't be expected to come in knowing everything. Send resume or call Steve Brooks, WEEO, Box 122, Waynesboro, PA 17268. (717) 762-3138.

AIR TALENT / Music Director wanted now for KXRX, Box 167, San Jose, CA 95103. T & R or call (408) 279-1738.

IS 6 TO 10 YOUR SHIFT? It just might be if rock 'n roll is your format. If you're interested in this evening air slot, write or call J.R. Greeley, KEWI, Box 4407, Topeka, KS 66604.

Figure 14-2 Employment newsletter. *(Courtesy Job Leads.)*

Look to the future—not only yours, but that of the broadcasting industry itself. What changes can and will be made in programming in the next several years? What new equipment will come onto the market, and how will it affect the business? What social trends will broadcasters need to become aware of? If you can anticipate the answers to these

questions you are on your way to becoming a professional radio broadcaster.

SUMMARY

The opportunities for a career in broadcasting are as good as they are in
any other field. There is always room for good, qualified people. One
advantage you may have is that a great many unqualified people are also
trying to get into broadcasting. The person with talent and ability will
clearly stand out from the rest. Consider that you are competing with
many others, and remember that you have to make your application
stand out from the rest. Take some care with your résumé; prepare a
good audition tape. The rest is a matter of perseverance. If you have a
professional attitude you can become a professional broadcaster.

TERMINOLOGY

Audition tape   Telescoping music
Résumé   Union scale

ACTIVITIES

1 Prepare an audition tape and a résumé. Have a friend or a classmate play the
   role of a station manager who reads the résumé, listens to the tape, and
   interviews you. See if any questions are asked that you have trouble answering.
2 Contact teachers and former employers, and see if they will write letters of
   recommendation for you. Ask them if you can use them for references.
3 Make a package that contains your résumé, letters of recommendation, copy
   you have written, and an audition tape. Duplicate everything before you send
   it out.
4 Practice doing spontaneous auditions. It is entirely possible that this may be
   thrown at you when you apply for a job. Sometimes employers would rather
   hear what you can do on the spot rather than listen to an audition tape that
   you have prepared in advance.

Glossary

Actuality Voice of a person directly involved in a news story
Ad lib Unprepared and spontaneous comments
Affiliate A station that has contracted to carry network programs
AFTRA American Federation of Television and Radio Artists
Airwaves Popular term for radio transmission
Ampere The measuring unit for current
Amplitude The high and low points of a sine wave
AOR Album-oriented rock
Ascertainment The investigation made by a broadcaster to learn the needs of a
    community
Attributive phrase The phrase at the end of a quotation that tells who said it
Audio console See Console
Audio equipment Equipment that processes sound and sound voltages
Audio feed A spoken message received via wire or radio transmission
Audition A tryout of speech or other performance to determine acceptability
Back announce To announce the name of a record after it has been played
Back timing Timing a record so that it will end exactly at the time desired

BBC British Broadcasting Corporation

Bidirectional mike A microphone that picks up sound on two sides

Block programming Dividing the broadcast day into small segments—usually 15-, 30-, or 60-minute blocks

Board Audio console. See Console

Board fade Using volume control to turn down the sound

Book Periodic report prepared by audience survey companies

Broadcast endorsement Authorization for an individual to operate a broadcasting station

Broadcasting Sending radio messages to a broad, general audience

Bulk eraser An electromagnet used for quickly removing all the sound patterns from magnetic tape

Cardioid mike A directional microphone that picks up sound in a heart-shaped pattern

Carrier Radio frequency signal upon which audio sound frequencies are transmitted

Cart Abbreviation for tape cartridge

Cart machine Cartridge tape recorder or player

Chain break Station break or station identification given between programs

Channel Designated frequency upon which a broadcasting station operates

Citation A notice issued by the FCC that a broadcaster has violated a rule

Class A time Preferred broadcasting time, when station has the most listeners

Combo Combination announcer and engineer

Communicaster Host on a radio talk show

Composite week Days of the week selected by the FCC to determine the quality of programming done by the broadcasting station during the term of its license

Condenser mike A type of microphone in which one or both plates of an electrical condenser vibrate to produce audio voltages

Console The main section of audio control to which all other studio equipment is connected; also called a "board" or "mixer"

Construction permit A document issued by the FCC permitting construction or modification of broadcast equipment

CPB Corporation for Public Broadcasting

Cross fade To fade out of one audio source and into another

Cross talk Sound voltages picked up by induction from one channel that interfere with the sound voltages in another channel

Cue An indication to start. Also, finding the point on a record or tape where the sound begins

Cumes Abbreviation for cumulative ratings, indicating the number of people listening to a station in a given period of time

Current The flow of electricity, measured in amperes

Dead air A period of time when there is no sound being transmitted

Decibel The measurement unit for sound level

Demographics Sociological characteristics of a segment of the population

Direct address   Using radio transmission to talk directly to a particular individual

Direct quote   Repeating the exact words spoken by another person

Directional mike   A microphone that picks up sound mainly from one direction. Same as unidirectional microphone

Disclaimer   An announcement to the effect that opinions expressed are not necessarily those of the station

Distortion   Any difference between the original sound and reproduced sound

Double spotting   Scheduling two spot announcements in immediate succession

Drive time   Morning and afternoon hours when people are commuting to and from work

Dual operation   Two-person operation, one announcing and one engineering

Dubbing   Duplicating sound, usually from one tape to another

Dynamic mike   A type of microphone in which a coil of wire vibrates to produce audio voltages

EBS   Emergency Broadcast System

Enunciation   Clarity in speaking

ET   Electrical transcription. Voice or music recorded on a disk in individual, separated tracks. Usually a series of short spot announcements

Extemporize   Elaborating spontaneously around a prepared message

Fader   Volume control. Also called a "pot"

Fairness Doctrine   Policy of the FCC that requires broadcasting stations to deal fairly with controversial issues

FCC   Federal Communications Commission

Feedback   Squeal or howl produced by sound coming from a loudspeaker, reentering the microphone, and recirculating the chain of transmission to the speaker

First Phone   First Class Radiotelephone Operator's License

Format   Sequence of programs, recorded music, and announcements

Free-speech message   A message written and spoken by a private citizen expressing his own viewpoint

Frequency   The number of cycles per second of a sine wave; also, colloquially, the "spot on the dial" where a station operates

Frequency discount   A discount given to an advertiser based upon the number of spot announcements purchased

Fringe area   Area where a broadcasting station is received only faintly

Gain   Volume

High impedance   High load resistance. Characteristic of non-professional audio equipment

Hot clock   The face of a clock labeled to indicate the times that certain types of records are to be played

IBEW   International Brotherhood of Electrical Workers

IBS   Intercollegiate Broadcasting System

Impedance   The electrical load imposed by one piece of equipment upon another to which it is connected

Independent station   A broadcasting station not affiliated with a network

Indirect quote   Paraphrase of the words spoken by another person

Induction   The generation of an electromotive force in a conductor from another conductor insulated from the first

Initial sound   Sound at the beginning of a word

Input   Information or sound fed into a communications system; the electrical point in equipment at which signal voltage is applied

Institutional promotion   Campaign to publicize the name of an organization so that it will be recognized and remembered, with little or no effort to promote the sale of specific products or services

IPS   Inches per second

Jack   Female electrical connector. Socket

Kill date   Termination date of a spot announcement

Kilo   Thousand

Kilocycle   Thousand cycles per second. Same as kilohertz

Lavalier mike   A microphone that is hung around the neck

Lead   The beginning paragraph of a news story

Lead in   The sentences that prepare the listener for a news report

Level   Volume of sound as indicated on a volume unit meter

Line-in jack   Input socket for high-level (amplified) signals

Live copy   Copy that is read directly on the air rather than being prerecorded

Load   A piece of equipment that draws electric current

Logs   Daily records of programs or performance of broadcasting equipment

Low impedence   Low load resistance. Characteristic of professional audio equipment

Master control   A room that contains all the audio equipment necessary for broadcasting

Megahertz   Million cycles per second

Middle sounds   The phonemes in the middle of a word

Milliamp   One one-thousandth of an ampere

Mixer   A unit that can control individually the volume of microphones and other audio equipment connected to it. See Console

Modulation   Variation in frequency or amplitude of a radio frequency carrier by sound; voice, music, or sound that is amplified or reproduced by audio equipment

Monitor   To listen to and check program quality. Also, the speaker or headset used to hear the amplified sound

MOR   Middle-of-the-road. Pertaining to popular music

Music under   Music, usually recorded, played under the voice of the announcer

NAB   National Association of Broadcasters

NABET   National Association of Broadcast Engineers and Technicians

National rep   A representative contracted to a broadcasting station to obtain national advertising accounts

Network   Any arrangement made by several stations to broadcast programs simultaneously

Nondirectional mike A microphone whose sensitivity is the same from all directions

NPR National Public Radio

Off mike Speaking too far away from a microphone, or into a side that is not "live"

Ohm The measuring unit for resistance

Omnidirectional mike Same as nondirectional mike

Out Communication is ended and no response is necessary

Out cue The last word of a spoken message or report. A cue for the next program element to begin

Output The information or sound that comes out of a communications system. Also, the point at which the sound comes out of the equipment

Pacing Rate at which a message or program proceeds

Participating advertiser An advertiser who buys spot announcements on a broadcasting station but does not control the program content

Patch cord A cord that connects two pieces of equipment in a communications system

Patch panel A bank of jacks used to interconnect pieces of equipment in a communications system by means of patch cords

Payola Money paid illegally to broadcast personnel in return for favors

Peak The high point registered by the needle on a VU meter

Phone patch Device or circuitry that connects a telephone to an audio system for recording or further transmission

Phonetic Alphabet, International The standard set of symbols representing the sounds produced in human speech

Play list A list compiled by the disk jockey of the records played on the air

Plug Male electrical connector

Point-to-point communication See Direct address

Potentiometer A volume control device. Also called a "pot"

Power The work that is done by an electric circuit, measured in watts

Primer Document issued by the FCC to explain a rule or concept promulgated by the Commission

Prime time The time of day when a broadcasting station has its largest listening audience

Program log Daily record of all programs and spot announcements broadcast by a station. Required by the FCC

Project To speak with strong volume and clear enunciation

Promo An announcement promoting a program or activity of the station

Proof of performance Measurements of power and frequency verifying that a station has been operating within its designated parameters

Protection Separating commercial announcements that are in competition with each other so that they are not heard too close together

PSA Public service announcement

Public file A compilation of license applications, construction permits, ascertainment reports, correspondence with the FCC, letters from the public, proof of performance, and other matter pertaining to the operation of a broadcasting station which the public is entitled to inspect

Quadraphonic Sound picked up through four different channels and transmitted simultaneously on one FM carrier

Radiotelephone Communications system in which a radio frequency carrier is modulated by sound; a wireless system which uses a microphone rather than a telegraph key for communication

Rate card Brochure printed and distributed by a broadcasting station which lists the costs of advertising at various times of the day

Rating Statistical percentages indicating the size of a station's listening audience

Remote A program originating away from the broadcasting studio

Residuals Payment to an announcer or other performer, made on the basis of the number of times a recorded spot announcement is aired

Resistance A load put upon an electric circuit, measured in ohms

Résumé A summary of an individual's qualifications for employment

Ribbon mike A type of microphone in which a thin strip of metal, vibrating in a magnetic field, produces sound voltages.

Rip-and-read Derogatory term referring to the practice of reading copy from a wire service with little or no rephrasing or editing

Rules and Regulations Publication issued in three volumes by the FCC to provide legal parameters for broadcasting stations

Saturation In broadcast advertising, the practice of making a large "buy" of air time, usually on several stations, for a short period of time, to promote a sale or activity

SC Station continuity. Announcement promoting an activity of the station

Segue (SEG-way) To go from one program item to another without an announcement in between

Set A group of records segued together

Share Statistical percentage indicating the size of a station's listening audience in proportion to that of the other stations in the area

Shotgun mike A highly directional microphone (having a very narrow pickup pattern) that will focus on sound coming from a point a considerable distance away

Signal The radio frequency emission of a broadcasting station. Also sound voltages and currents

Simulcasting Broadcasting the same program on two stations simultaneously, as by an AM and an FM station operated by the same owners, or as a collaboration between a television station and an FM station, to provide a telecast—of a symphonic concert, for example—with stereo sound

Sine wave A curve that represents the flow of alternating current

Sound In broadcast jargon, program content and overall style of a broadcasting station. May also be called the "format"

SP Station promotion. See SC

Sponsor Advertiser who provides financial backing for all or part of a broadcasting program

Spot   An announcement, either commercial or public service

Standard broadcast   AM radio

Stringer   Part-time news reporter who gets paid by the story or by the word

Tag   Live ending to a recorded spot. Additional information, usually of a local or timely nature

Talent fee   Payment to an announcer or other performer

Target audience   Specific population segment which a broadcasting station attempts to reach

Telescoping   Squeezing together words or music. In speaking, the contracting of sounds of words. Also, cutting out the middle portion of a musical selection to shorten the time of the music

TFN   Till further notice

Top 40   The forty most popular records of the current week. Also a station that plays only the most popular records

Trade journal   Periodical serving a particular industry or profession

Trade-out   Exchanging advertising for products or services

Traffic director   The person responsible for putting into the log all the programs and spot announcements scheduled for every broadcast day

Underwriting   The granting of funds to a noncommercial station to aid in its financial support. FCC policy permits a simple, noncommercial, on-the-air acknowledgment of such grants

Unidirectional microphone   A microphone that picks up sound mainly from one direction. Same as directional microphone

Union scale   A rate of pay for specified work agreed to by a union

Voice-over   Talking over music or sound

Volt   The measuring unit for voltage

Voltage   Electromotive force, measured in volts

VU meter   Volume unit meter. A meter that registers the volume of sound in modulation percentage and in decibels

Watt   The measuring unit for power

Windscreen   A sound-transparent cover placed over a microphone to minimize the distorting effect of wind and certain speech sounds

Wire service   An organization that distributes news and other written copy to subscribers by means of teletype

Woodshedding   Reading over the copy prior to the time it is to be read on the air

Zero level   One hundred percent modulation, as measured by a VU meter

Bibliography

General Background and Information

Cole, Barry and Mal Oettinger, *Reluctant Regulators* (Reading, Mass.: Addison-Wesley, 1978)

Coleman, Howard, *Case Studies in Broadcast Management: Radio and TV* (New York: Hastings House, 1978)

Foster, Eugene S., *Understanding Broadcasting* (Reading, Mass.: Addison-Wesley, 1978)

Head, Sydney W., *Broadcasting in America, 2d ed.* (Boston: Houghton Mifflin, 1972)

Kahn, Frank J. (ed.), *Documents of American Broadcasting* (Englewood Cliffs, N.J.: Prentice-Hall, 1973)

Johnson, Joseph S. and Kenneth K. Jones, *Modern Radio Station Practices* (Belmont, Calif.: Wadsworth, 1972)

Robinson, Sol, *Broadcast Station Operation Guide* (Blue Ridge Summit: Tab Books, 1968)

Broadcast Journalism

Bittner, John R. and Denise A. Bittner, *Radio Journalism* (Englewood Cliffs, N.J.: Prentice-Hall, 1977)

Bliss, Edward Jr. and John M. Patterson, *Writing News for Broadcast* (New York: Columbia, 1971)

Smeyak, Paul G., *Broadcast News Writing* (Columbus: Grid, Inc., 1977)

Tankard, Jr. and Michael Ryan, *Basic News Reporting* (Palo Alto: Mayfield Publishing Company, 1977)

Studio Production

Hybels, Saundra, and Dana Ulloth, *Broadcasting: An Introduction to Radio and Television* (Princeton: Van Nostrand, 1978)

Seidle, Ronald J. *Air Time* (Boston: Holbrook Press, 1977)

Announcing

Hyde, Stuart W., *Television and Radio Announcing* (Boston: Houghton Mifflin 1971)

License Handbooks

Broadcast Operator Handbook (Washington: Federal Communications Commission Field Operations Bureau, 1976)

McKenzie, Alexander A., *Radiotelephone Examination Key and Answers* (New York: McGraw-Hill, 1972)

Noll, Edward M., *Third Class Radiotelephone License Handbook* (New York: Bobbs-Merrill, 1976)

Schwartz, Martin, *Commercial Radio Operator's License Guide* (Williston Park, N.Y.: Ameco Publishing Corporation, 1975)

Index

Index